THEATER
and the
ADOLESCENT ACTOR

THEATER

and the

ADOLESCENT ACTOR

BUILDING A SUCCESSFUL
SCHOOL PROGRAM

Camille L. Poisson

ARCHON BOOKS · 1994

© 1994 Camille L. Poisson. All rights reserved.
First published 1994 as an Archon Book,
an imprint of The Shoe String Press, Inc.
Hamden, Connecticut 06514.

Library of Congress Cataloging-in-Publication Data
Poisson, Camille L., 1948–
Theater and the adolescent actor : building
a successful school program / Camille L. Poisson.
p. cm.
Includes bibliographical references.
1. College and school drama, American.
2. Amateur theater—United States—Production and direction.
3. Acting—Study and teaching—United States.
4. Youth as actors—United States. I. Title.
PN3178.P7P65   1994   93-36406   792'.0222'071273—dc20
ISBN 0-208-02380-1 (alk. paper).

The paper used in this publication meets the minimum
requirements of American National Standard for
Information Sciences—Permanence of Paper for
Printed Library Materials, ANSI Z39.48-1984. ∞

Printed in the United States of America

*To the memory of Leonard J. Riendeau,
a teacher, colleague, and friend.*

CONTENTS

PART IV   Teaching Basics

PART V   The Play Production Process

Appendixes

PREFACE

This book grew out of my experience as a secondary school drama teacher, and my work as a master teacher and supervisor of practice teachers from the Emerson College Theater Department. I wanted to write about the realities and challenges of teaching drama in the public school setting, and to provide insight into the inner workings of the public school and how the drama teacher fits in.

This book is not intended as the last word on how to teach drama and produce plays. Rather it is intended as an introductory guide to developing a solid secondary level drama program. Its aim is to show trained professionals how to function effectively in the public school environment, and how to meet the needs of the adolescent as both student and performer.

The success of any school theater program greatly depends on the teacher's ability to get a positive response to theater in the school environment. This book details the various roles a drama teacher must play in order to stimulate and maintain student interest, as well as to generate the community, administrative, and staff support—both moral and financial—essential to a drama program. It also provides professional tips for overcoming teaching problems basic to the public school setting.

Since adolescents relate to dramatics differently at the various stages of their development, this book points out behavioral changes typical of each age group and introduces ways to adapt to them all. In addition, it shows you how to structure various types of drama courses and how to adjust your teaching approach to each grade level.

Because producing plays for public performance is a large part of most junior and senior high school drama programs, I have provided a step-by-step guide for structuring and organizing the entire process *within the school framework,* including how to:

1. Staff and manage a student production company and find the most qualified students for each staff position.
2. Maximize rehearsal time and stretch your production budget.
3. Solve production problems using available school and community resources.
4. Prepare students for production week without disrupting their school routine.

For the teaching insights that served as the basis of this book, I am indebted to all of the junior and senior high school students I have had the pleasure of teaching over the years. They have proved to me over and over again the indefatigability and creative potential of youth, and have showed me that anything is possible. Thanks are particularly due to Myra Slotnick, who, during the course of my writing, kept me focused on the "student perspective" and helped fill in any memory gaps on production details and procedures. Finally, I wish to thank my husband, Leslie, for his helpful advice, editorial assistance, and undying support.

Part I

THE DRAMA TEACHER

Many of the biggest advances in civilization have been the chief work, not of politicians or inventors, not even of artists, but of teachers.

—Gilbert Highet,
The Art of Teaching

1

Roles, Goals, and Responsibilities

Many of you are at the beginning of what will hopefully be a rewarding career in teaching. But let's face it: teaching is hard work, and it's difficult to ignore the plight of today's public schools. Limited funding for the arts is a reality and may discourage the best trained teachers. But no matter what you've read or what you've been told, remember this: whether or not a school has the best books or the best facilities, teaching is what *you* make it and what *you* bring to it. It's not *where* you teach but *how* you teach that's important. Making the most of what you have, creating more with less, is more often than not the main challenge of the secondary school drama teacher.

Before we get into all the practical specifics of finances, teaching methods, and the drama teacher's place in the secondary school, however, we need to understand what teaching drama at this level is all about. There are many roles, goals, and responsibilities involved—some more obvious, others more difficult—but all are important.

No doubt your primary goal is to awaken young people to the magic and marvel of theater. You must find ingenious ways to spark interest and stimulate creativity. Being part of a production company can have a positive and lasting effect on a young person's life. Your job is to immerse students in *every* facet of the production process and teach them the necessary skills.

But the work doesn't stop there. A drama teacher should also teach students about the cultural benefits of theater and its value in society. Exposing your students to theater history and dramatic literature allows them to examine different cultures, philosophies, and values. By instilling adolescents with an appreciation for theater as a creative voice, as a vehicle for presenting ideas and different points of view, you help them gain insight into themselves and the world around them.

A large part of this process involves making theater *fun*. Use all the techniques of a performer to grab hold of your audience, to connect with your students, and to infuse them with energy and enthusiasm. You will often feel like a commedia dell'arte performer—an improvisational actor facing a class with nothing more than a lesson plan as a guide, working hard to enliven your subject and stimulate response. Some days you'll hit the mark; other days you won't. It is always important to remember that you serve as the model for your craft. Unless a drama teacher projects the qualities of a theater professional, no lasting impression will be made. You must be both uninhibited and disciplined, just as you expect your students to be.

As an educator, your primary concern should be the personal growth and development of your students, *especially* when casting and producing plays. While a professional director has the luxury of working with trained actors, designers, and technicians, a drama teacher is limited to the available talent within a school. Do you seek out the most talented students, or do you strive to develop the talent of those less gifted? You can do both. As a teaching tool, play production has far more to do with molding character than with discovering future talent for the stage. If you are fortunate to have in your midst students who show great promise, consider them *gifts*. Yet never neglect students whose talents require time and patience to develop, nor pass over those who have little promise but are willing and eager to participate. Make room for all levels of skills and allow students to develop and use whatever abilities they have, whether acting on stage or working behind the scenes.

A drama teacher's greatest satisfaction comes from working with adolescents who apply themselves and do their best, regardless of their level of talent. When students of this age are given an opportunity to contribute, to feel needed and be "part of the group," they develop a sense of worth and belonging few school experiences can provide. This is the real purpose of educational theater.

This does not mean you must sacrifice the quality of your productions, however. Training your students in professional theater skills and fostering their personal development are two goals that go hand in hand, for only by adhering to high standards in performance will students develop and grow. The result? High-quality productions, and young people who are far better for the experience.

Ultimately, a significant part of the drama experience involves the close interaction between teacher and students. As a result of this closeness, drama teachers often get to know their students better than other teachers do. This can be a blessing as well as a curse. The frequent emotional upsets of adolescence can easily affect a student's mood and work. And when one student's performance is affected, so is the performance of the group.

There will, therefore, be times when a drama teacher needs to counsel students, help them work out personal problems, or intercede in conflicts, especially when personality clashes or differences of opinion arise during the production process. Whether you're teaching a class or producing a play, a great deal of finesse is needed to handle and resolve these problems effectively.*

If students come to you for advice or help, be supportive and sensitive to their needs. Don't lecture or prejudge—nothing will turn them off more quickly. Learn to be a good listener. Never tell students what to do—provide options and choices instead. In this way they will learn to make their own decisions, and they'll respect you for giving them the chance. But above all, remember that adolescents are highly impressionable. Any advice or opinion you offer can influence the way they deal with life's experiences both now and in the future. This is a responsibility no teacher should take lightly.

Educational theater involves teaching basic life skills. By stimulating creative thinking and problem solving, you not only show students how to conceptualize and execute ideas, you also teach the importance of personal commitment, cooperative work, and goal setting. As a mentor, you have the responsibility of integrating sound philosophical and ethical principles into your teaching, and providing students with sensible values that will help them grow and develop into well-adjusted, productive adults.

When you broaden their horizons, they discover choices they never thought available. When you heighten their awareness of the world, they discover opportunities they didn't know existed. You will not only earn their respect, but in time, if you care enough, their gratitude and appreciation as well. These are the rewards of teaching secondary school drama, and they can make all your hard work and perseverance worthwhile.

---

* Sometimes you'll require assistance in dealing with more serious behavior problems. It's important to seek the help of school counselors and psychologists in dealing with truancy, unreliability, compulsive lying or stealing, or violent behavior of any kind. It goes without saying that criminal behavior should be immediately reported to the proper authorities.

2

What It Takes to Be Effective

Although all drama teachers share many of the same goals, roles, and responsibilities, every teacher is different and brings something unique to her teaching. What qualities and methods make a better, more effective teacher?

A good drama teacher should enjoy working with adolescents, be genuinely committed to teaching, and be willing to develop an honest relationship with students. An adolescent will respond positively to a teacher who respects him as an individual, acknowledges his uniqueness, and has his best interests at heart.

But have no illusions. Drawing out and nurturing young talent demands a great deal of patience and discipline. You must be uncompromising in your standards, unyielding in your expectations, and willing to put in the time and effort to get results. Knowing your craft is never enough. You must also be prepared to assume a variety of teaching tasks. Creating and organizing courses, budgeting and purchasing books and materials, and developing and managing a theater program are as much a part of teaching as directing and producing plays.

You'll also need to be aware of how your students perceive you; strangely enough, this will also determine your effectiveness. Most adolescents respond well to teachers who believe in what they teach and who approach their subject with confidence and assertiveness. If you don't love your subject or believe it worthwhile, neither will your students. Remember, adolescents read their teachers instantly, and will easily detect insecurity or insincerity. They also won't hesitate to turn your habits and idiosyncrasies into labels or nicknames (do "Snake," "Patton," or "Old Stoneface" ring a bell?). Unfortunately, this is the nature of the adolescent beast—hard to fool, and quick to judge. A good first impression is of primary importance.

To be effective, you must also be dynamic and flexible in your approach. Since adolescents constantly ride the emotional roller coaster of puberty, be prepared to adapt to their changes in behavior and be willing to accept the roles of counselor, disciplinarian, or supportive mentor. Challenge students at every opportunity and allow them freedom to grow, but always within well-established boundaries. Keep in mind, however, that your ground rules and disciplinary actions should emanate from a desire to help students develop, and *not* from a need to dominate or control. Avoid being dictatorial or authoritarian. This will only result in rebellious and resentful behavior and destroy any chance of establishing an open teacher/student relationship.

Bridging the generational gap is a constant challenge. Adolescents are wary of adults and may perceive them as dull; adults, on the other hand, may find adolescents' behavior . . . well, *adolescent*. A sense of humor is essential. Humor is an effective tool in showing the young that not everyone over twenty-one is dead. At the same time, it helps a teacher see adolescent childishness for what it really is: awkwardness, ready to be penetrated and dissolved. Humor, therefore, creates a common ground for understanding and an atmosphere of togetherness. And this togetherness is fundamental to teaching. (See Gilbert Highet's *The Art of Teaching*, p. 57; Mr. Highet has an excellent discussion of the qualities of a good teacher.)

Humor will also lower student defenses. Show students how to laugh at themselves and how to see uncomfortable performance situations in a more humorous light. Introduce drama activities that are enjoyable and easily accomplished. Exposing students to performance situations where they feel comfortable builds their confidence and leaves them eager to forge ahead with new challenges.

Your main job as a teacher is to communicate information and be sure it is understood. When questions are raised, bring them up again later in a different context so students can fully process and understand issues, theories, or different aspects of the subject. Remember the bright student who has presented a good illustration or a creative idea, and call on that student again in the future. Also remember the quiet student who has difficulty grasping concepts. Take time to present illustrative anecdotes to ensure a mental connection is made.

Teachers should also be able to correlate facts and information. If theater is truly a reflection of society, there is little value in teaching theater history or dramatic literature unless a linkage is made to the people, beliefs, and social systems of the historical times. Isolated dates and events have no meaning. An effective teacher will make a point of showing how apparently remote facts are relevant and organically linked. This is important, for adolescents tend to take much of what they learn and compartmentalize it in their minds for the sole purpose of spewing it back later, in tests, quizzes, or term papers. A good teacher will help students dissect, examine, and make sense of information so that it can be integrated into their thinking and practically applied (Highet, pp. 58–59).

Finally, it is of paramount importance for a teacher to be a constant source of encouragement. Whenever students are frustrated or discouraged, be there to point out and reinforce their qualities and strengths; convince them that shortcomings or bad experiences are always fuel for growth. By being sensitive to their needs and never underestimating their potential, you can help adolescents develop a sense of worth, a sense of pride, and a sense of accomplishment that will ultimately make *you* a better person and a more effective teacher.

If, after serious reflection and soul searching, you believe you have what it takes and feel you can make a difference, then you're ready for the next step: finding the job that is right for you.

3

The Job Market: Hard Realities and Hidden Opportunities

Theater's place in the secondary school curriculum varies from system to system. Performing arts high schools and large city magnet schools are unique because they generally offer drama as a major. However, most traditional junior and senior high schools treat theater as an extracurricular activity or as an elective. The status of drama at your school will, of course, directly affect the scope of your job in terms of teaching responsibilities and work hours.

Most rural, suburban, and inner-city schools offering drama as an extracurricular activity often have limited budgets, and rely on an energetic, well-intentioned faculty member—who may or may not have theater training—to direct plays or run a drama club. Many hire a qualified drama teacher on a part-time basis to run an after-school activity. In order to find a *full-time* job in a school with this type of program, you must be certified to teach another curriculum course, such as speech or English (for information on your state's licensing requirements, contact your local school board), and be willing to run a theater activity after school. Where the average teacher works a seven-hour day, it is not unusual for a drama teacher to put in ten. You will essentially work two jobs, while your salary reflects only one.

Many secondary schools offer separate contracts for extracurricular activities. But salaries, which vary greatly, are generally based on the program's value to a community. Although well-funded after-school programs exist (usually in

11

wealthy communities), school committees tend to place greater value on sports than on theater, and are willing to pay a teacher far more for coaching (as much as five times more) than for producing plays—even though longer hours and a larger number of students are involved.

This type of position has obvious shortcomings, but there are hidden opportunities and advantages worth noting. When you teach *any* related course, you're often in a position to expose students to theater through your classes. If you teach speech, incorporate a few units of drama, or set up the course to include drama one or two days a week; if you teach art, include a unit or two of costume and set design; if you teach shop, incorporate a unit of stagecraft. Adding variety to a course always makes it more appealing.

If the subject is English, you may not have the same flexibility in structuring a course, but what you *can* do is include plays in your reading list, and expose students to the performance situation at every opportunity. Instead of reading a play in class, have them act out roles using props and minimal sets; assign oral rather than written book reports. This will not only sharpen students' public speaking skills, but will also help you spot acting potential for a school play.

There is one great advantage to teaching English: you have access to more students, and therefore a larger source to tap for plays. Because English is a required subject, you also have more academic clout to induce students to participate in drama. Students who have no dramatic experience are often reluctant to try out for a production on their own. But when you make the production part of a required course, they're more likely to get involved, even if only to improve their grade. You can provide incentives by offering extra credit to students who audition, and additional credit if they make the play or get involved in production work. Require those who choose not to participate to write a review of the play. This will give the additional benefit of a guaranteed audience. In the process some students may discover they don't like theater, while others may become addicted. In either case, they'll be exposed to a new and different experience.

No matter what curriculum subject you teach, don't be afraid to create your *own* opportunities. In my first teaching job, I was hired to teach speech and direct the senior class play. Speech was a half-year requirement for all sophomore English students. I taught five speech classes each day and ran a weekly one-hour drama activity period open to all students. Because I made drama an integral part of my courses, many sophomores developed a genuine interest in theater and were unwilling to wait until their senior year to be involved in a production. They were eager for the kind of experience that neither a meager one-hour drama activity period nor a speech course could provide. So with the help of a young and enthusiastic chorus teacher and a very dedicated shop teacher, we produced the school's first full-scale musical. Having no budget for materials, we scavenged for everything. Although the show didn't turn a profit, I did gain invaluable teaching and directing experience, as well as the students' gratitude and appreciation. The real bonus was earning the approval of the principal, who helped me obtain funding for subsequent productions.

Rural, suburban, and inner-city schools with extracurricular drama programs are a wonderful training ground because you're forced to be creative in the way you incorporate theater into a curriculum course and in the way you stimulate student interest in theater; you also become a master at producing plays on a shoe string. Don't be too quick to dismiss this kind of teaching position. The most desired positions, however, are found in schools where drama is a curriculum subject. Many drama electives are offered through the English department, while others are offered through a separate drama department, or as part of a fine arts department that includes art and music. As a subject, drama may be a full-year general theater course, or a series of individual semester- or mini-courses in specific areas of theater, i.e. dramatic literature, acting, theater history, or play production.

In terms of teaching opportunities and creative freedom, the ideal jobs are always found in schools that hire one full-time drama teacher who reports only to the principal. With complete autonomy over the program, you teach a full load of courses of your own design, and you are in charge of your own budget. You have the freedom to decide what books and materials to purchase, and the luxury of deciding the number and types of plays to produce, as well as the direction of the program.

On the other hand, teaching in a large suburban or regional high school with a large drama department has other advantages, namely, a larger budget and better facilities. But you are just one of a number of drama teachers under the supervision of a department head. With a set curriculum to follow, your creative ideas and course innovations undergo closer scrutiny. You're also obliged to attend department meetings to discuss curriculum improvements and play selections. Having less autonomy, you're expected to share teaching and directing responsibilities. You do, however, have the luxury of teaching theater full-time.

Potential teaching jobs come in many forms and under many guises at the secondary level. The key is to find ways to incorporate drama into classroom teaching—whether you're using established drama courses, or creating your own course, or integrating theater into an existing related course. Job satisfaction ultimately depends on the time and effort you're willing to put into exposing young people to theater, and on the strength of your desire to teach.

Part II

THE DRAMA PROGRAM

Imagination is more important than knowledge.
—Albert Einstein

4

The Purpose of Drama
in Education

All would agree that a secondary school education should prepare young people for adulthood and help them become functioning members of society. To that end, students should be given the basic tools for competing and succeeding in life, and provided with meaningful, fulfilling experiences. The study of drama does this and much more.

Through acting, adolescents learn to interpret and communicate ideas and feelings by means of skits, improvisations, and scene work. By developing roles, they learn to explore their feelings through emotional recall and introspection. Through acting, they become focused and more physically aware. Although the discipline and concentration required can be tedious and intense, there is a breakthrough, and it comes when the student first experiences the actor/audience connection and realizes its powerful effect.

In performing, students blossom, and quickly shed their inhibitions. They open emotionally, express their thoughts more freely, and communicate more efficiently. With increased self-confidence and self-worth, they begin to realize the value of their talents and of their contribution to a group. And as they discover new possibilities, their goals and ambitions begin to crystalize.

The benefits of theater can be experienced in the classroom as well. The study of plays is a study of human nature, and helps adolescents understand man's view of himself and the constant change in his world. Theater history also alters and expands their view of society. Exposing students to social issues and attitudes of the past helps them understand cause and effect in their own world by showing how strongly individual beliefs influence society.

Even the technical aspects of theater can help prepare students for adult life. In the study of stagecraft and design, not only are practical skills acquired, but the ability to think creatively as well. In turn, executing ideas leads toward independence and self-reliance. The production experience teaches the importance of organization and cooperation in completing any given task. The student becomes decisive, learning to overcome obstacles and solve problems quickly and rationally.

Theater's effect on young people is long-lasting and takes many forms. For the uninspired student, the student with an apparent loss of direction, the student with few friends who doesn't quite fit in, theater can help in developing a sense of belonging, a sense of self, and a heightened self-esteem. For the serious academic student, the production experience provides a strong foundation for the development of leadership qualities. These, as well as the communication and organizational skills acquired, become assets in any chosen field or profession.

At times, the impact of theater on students of this age can be so startling and immediate that dramatic changes quickly develop. This happened with one of my students—a bright, handsome, popular star of the football team. Like many other high school boys, he considered theater and acting an activity for "wimps." In his senior year, however, he auditioned for the spring musical *on a dare*, and to his surprise was given a lead part. The experience was a revelation; he found acting so enjoyable that he decided to major in theater in college and eventually became a professional dancer, all because of this *one* experience. Stories like this are not uncommon.

Although some students pursue careers in theater as a result of their high school experience, drama's primary role in education is one of enrichment. A student's involvement and participation in theater, coupled with the strong bonds developed with fellow cast and crew members, evoke deep and lasting feelings—feelings that lead to further self-discovery and self-exploration.

Should drama be part of every secondary school curriculum? Absolutely. Why? Because it has the power to affect and change the course of a young person's life.

5

Developing Curriculum Courses

How then does one approach theater in the classroom? Theater can be approached as a craft, a visual art, a discipline, or simply as a recreational activity. No matter what your approach or what aspect of drama you teach, when designing courses for the secondary level, it's important to keep the following basic points in mind.

▶ **Point 1: A DRAMA COURSE SHOULD BE DEMANDING AS WELL AS ENJOYABLE.**

Although drama is commonly looked upon as a recreational subject by administrations and students alike, teaching theater effectively still requires structure and discipline. Adolescents have an aversion to anything that takes great effort and perseverance to accomplish; if they don't enjoy a class or see its purpose, they quickly lose interest. Whether a drama course is activity- or academically-oriented, its structure must allow students to express themselves creatively, and allow the teacher to channel that creativity in a productive manner.

Unfortunately, this is where many beginning teachers falter. If you always adhere strictly to lesson plans, students are often overwhelmed with too much material. A teacher whose main concern is to cover as much material as possible before the bell each day gets little feedback from a class. Without effective interaction with students, you'll not only become insensitive to their needs, but end up with bored students in a static teaching environment.

While some teachers lecture too much, others improvise too much. When your course lacks content and structure, you are in essence giving students free rein in the classroom. Students need creative freedom as well as encouragement in order to develop, but without proper direction and a solid foundation, creative ideas go nowhere.

For these reasons, courses need to be balanced: they should have substantive material and well-defined goals, but should also provide students the freedom to express themselves creatively and productively.

▶ **Point 2: LOW ENROLLMENT IN AN ELECTIVE SUBJECT CAN LEAD TO COURSE CANCELLATION.**

Because drama is an elective, it's important to draw as many students as possible. At this age, students rarely take a theater course solely for cultural enrichment. Those who sign up for drama simply to fulfill a credit requirement and who are not involved in a production often become isolated from the students who *are*; the subject matter becomes meaningless and the course more often than not is dropped.

For adolescents to develop and maintain an interest in theater, they must be continually motivated. And the best motivating tool is the school play. Involved students are more likely to enroll in future classes. To encourage students, establish a schedule of public productions and make participation mandatory, or at least an extra credit option. Make the school play the program core.

▶ **Point 3: THE BREADTH AND CONTENT OF A COURSE SHOULD BE GEARED TO THE MATURITY AND ABILITY LEVEL OF ADOLESCENTS.**

Learn to limit course information to an amount easily grasped by each age group. If students come in with background in theater, find out how much. Distribute a questionnaire on the first day of class to find out what drama classes each student has already taken, what plays they've been in or worked on, and what special skills or talents they may have. If your school has an existing drama program, check the curriculum guide, or contact the former drama teacher about how courses were set up and what material was covered. Knowing from the start what to include or delete from a course will help you avoid the painful process of trial and error in meeting the needs and experience level of your students.

When creating courses in a school where no previous drama program existed, follow two steadfast rules. First, begin with theater basics. This can include theater games, acting exercises, theater and acting terms, stage direction, play production, or any other aspect of theater deemed appropriate. The younger the students, the more elementary your subject material. Second, make the material relevant. If students feel overwhelmed, or don't see relevancy in what they're being taught, they may not continue with drama in the future. Always present your material in a way that best helps students visualize and understand the subject.

This is especially important when teaching the more abstract concepts and theories of theater. For example, because the adolescent's main association with acting is television and movies, Stanislavski's concept of characterization can be taught using well-known characters from either of these mediums as examples.

When introducing a class to different types of drama, refer to TV programs or films most familiar to students to illustrate each genre. Theater purists of course will argue that teaching this lesson accurately requires nothing less than the study of representative plays. Granted. But your primary goal here is to make sure students are able to understand and relate to the subject material. You can therefore make this concession whenever you find it necessary to keep the subject matter relevant. Once the basic concept is fully grasped by students, you can introduce subject material that is more appropriate to a specific lesson.

It's important to see a lesson from the students' point of view. Make it simple enough to understand. Simplifying course content does not mean diminishing quality. Always maintain high standards in what you expect from students, no matter what their academic level or maturation stage.

Be aware of the adolescent's perspective and use it to your advantage. Discover the likes and dislikes of each age group. Learn their social habits. Find out what movies appeal to them, what TV programs they faithfully watch, who their idols and heroes are. Build your students' knowledge of theater on what they already know.

▶ **Point 4: THE GREATER THE NUMBER OF DRAMA COURSES OFFERED, THE MORE COMPREHENSIVE AND SPECIALIZED THEY SHOULD BE.**

Make sure the courses you create from one grade to the next show a gradual progression in their degree of difficulty and in the amount of information covered, and that the courses are structured appropriately for the given age group.

At the junior high level, an activity-oriented course works best for two reasons. First, a recreational course is a good emotional outlet for this high energy group. Second, students of this age enjoy learning by doing. The best way to introduce subject matter at this level is to use activities to *reinforce* the facts. Here's an example: you're teaching stage direction. The students, however, are having trouble remembering the difference between upstage left and downstage right. Your first reaction is to pass out a mimeographed sheet of a floor plan indicating the different stage areas, and then ask students to memorize it. Fine. But a more effective and enjoyable way to teach this lesson is to test each student *on stage* by having them walk to the different stage areas as you call them out. To the student, the first approach is only another boring assignment, while the second is a game.

Although activity-oriented courses work well at both levels, senior high drama courses should be more academically challenging. A good introductory high school course should provide students an overview of different aspects of theater. A general course might include a unit or two on play production and acting, a unit on the different genres and styles of drama, a unit on selected plays from major literary periods, and a unit highlighting the major periods in theater history. Or, develop a series of concentrated courses focusing on one specific area at a time.

For example, in one school system, I ran both the junior and senior high drama programs; although they ran independently, I put together a six year program that covered the full scope of theater from grades seven through twelve. Each grade course offered more than the year before in terms of course content and production experience. In this way drama students were able to look forward to learning something new the following year.

My seventh grade course introduced students to the world of theater. In designing the course I wanted to impress upon these young minds the idea that drama could be fun. Since most students at this age have little or no background in theater, I wanted their first year of drama to be geared to creative exploration through creative dramatics and to making theater enjoyable so they'd want to continue in the program. The course was made up solely of theater games and two in-class workshop productions. The plays I selected were thirty-five to forty-five minutes long, and could be rehearsed and performed during a single class period. Students worked cooperatively in acquiring costumes, sets, and props.

The eighth grade course was expanded to include two in-class workshop productions, but emphasized the organizational aspect of a production. What had the year before been a simple delegation of duties on a voluntary basis now became a legitimate study and assignment of production staff positions and duties. Students were also given in-class projects and regular homework. By the time these students reached high school, they were able to handle the production and aesthetic aspects of theater in greater detail, and were assigned more responsibilities and more intensive course work.

Freshmen were exposed to every aspect of play production through hands-on work and participation in workshop productions. Sophomores were offered a concentrated course in acting that helped develop better skills through more advanced theater exercises, extensive scene work, and homework assignments. Students were also exposed to various acting theories and techniques, and were shown how different styles and forms of drama relate to acting.

Juniors were offered a comprehensive course on the craft and art of theater including stagecraft, lighting, costumes, and makeup, as well as history of theater and related plays. Seniors were given an advanced course on the aesthetics of theater involving in-depth study of the principles and elements of design, and were assigned projects in each design area. As a final project, seniors were required to complete a production book (play and character analysis, overall design concept, set and costume renderings, lighting plots, and floor plans) on a play or musical of their choice.

All high school drama students were required to put in thirty crew hours during the school year working on a department production in some technical capacity other than acting.

Anyone completing over thirty crew hours by the end of the year received extra credit points towards the final course grade.

Your goal is to develop courses that allow students to increase and expand their knowledge of theater from one school year to the next. (Sample course outlines are provided in appendix 1.)

▶ Point 5: GEAR A COURSE TO ONE AGE GROUP OR GRADE LEVEL.

When working with different age groups in one class, there may be enough difference in the maturity and experience level of students to hinder the effectiveness of a drama course. This is especially true in junior high. The maturation rate of adolescents between age twelve and fourteen varies *dramatically*. Rarely can seventh, eighth, and ninth graders be in the same drama class without creating serious interaction problems. So when possible, keep these age groups separate by creating a different drama course for each grade. And, *make sure* the guidance department schedules students accordingly.

If it is not possible to separate the grades, you can divide the class into groups and assign different theater projects and acting exercises according to students' ability and maturity. Or, involve them in a class production and select a play that has enough variety in the roles to challenge each age group. Consider placing the older, more experienced students in positions of authority. Make them group leaders in class projects and acting exercises, and crew heads in play production. Providing older students opportunities to serve as role models helps them develop a sense of responsibility, increases their self-confidence, and lessens their resentment for having to work with younger, less experienced students. Junior high drama classes having mixed age groups ultimately require more organization and flexibility in class activities and more diversity in subject matter than do unmixed classes.

Although maturation differences become less obvious once students reach high school, differences appear in the quality and depth of their work. Again, if you have a choice, create a separate high school course for each grade as well; if you don't, it will be necessary to allow students to work at their own level in terms of their acting ability, production experience, and technical skill, as well as their level of conceptual understanding of acting theories, theater concepts, and play production fundamentals. You will therefore need to be more subjective in evaluating the quality of individual work in a mixed-grade class.

▶ Point 6: SELL YOUR PROGRAM

To effectively implement courses in a school where no drama program exists often requires submitting a course of study for administrative approval. It's important to justify the need for such courses by emphasizing the educational worth of theater and its value in the curriculum. Your presentation should consist of a course of study including:

1. A statement of philosophy: the value and purpose of theater in education.
2. Educational goals: the outside objectives of drama, such as the development of social skills and cultural and aesthetic awareness.
3. General course objectives: how educational goals fit into the courses.
4. Title, description, and purpose of each course.
5. Unit plan for each course.

Each unit should include:

1. Unit title.
2. Unit overview. A summary of what the unit consists of in your own words.
3. Objectives of unit, including
   a. Subject matter to be learned.
   b. Specific skill objectives (getting students to read plays, to use their imaginations, to perform in front of a group, etc.).
   c. Skills students are expected to develop by learning the subject matter of the unit (body awareness, aesthetic and cultural appreciation, poise, public speaking skills, etc.).
4. Materials needed. These include visual aids, printed matter, and required textbooks.
5. Content of unit. State subject matter in outline form. For example:
   Unit I: Age of Realism
      a. *Study of and exposure to the method style of acting*
      b. *Study of the representational style of production*
      c. *Reading of notable American dramas*
      d. *Assigned scene preparation from notable scripts*
6. Methods of evaluation. State the testing methods used for measuring student comprehension and understanding of material covered. Also point out observation and evaluation methods to measure skills and work habits. Administrators must be convinced of a tangible form and sound basis for measuring and evaluating student growth and progress. This will often be the main selling point for including a theater arts program in the high school curriculum.

6

Working with a Limited Budget

Establishing a curriculum is the first step. But to teach theater effectively requires the proper tools—namely, books and materials. With such a wide variety of professional theater books on the market, how does a drama teacher decide which to buy and what types of books and materials are appropriate at the secondary level? What are the alternatives when money is limited?

Managing on a limited budget is one of the major challenges of the public school teacher, especially when selecting books and materials for the classroom. When purchasing books, think in terms of practicality, applicability, and physical durability. Any theater book used for high school teaching should a) cover the basics in one or more areas of theater, b) apply to different grade levels, and c) be reasonably priced.

If you're not quite sure what books to consider for students, or where to start, here are a few suggestions. Complete bibliographical information is provided at the back of this book (see Sources).

The Stage and the School, 5th edition, by Katharine Anne Ommanney and Harry H. Schanker, is a general classroom textbook used in many secondary schools today. The book covers all aspects of theater: the structure and varieties of drama, different forms of acting, highlights of various periods in theater history, and play production. It also provides excellent advice for producing and mounting high school musicals.

Fran Averett Tanner's *Basic Drama Projects*, 5th edition, is an excellent book for classroom teaching. It works well as both a student workbook and curriculum guide, providing a drama teacher with individual lessons, class activity sheets, and assignments on every aspect of theater, as well as a list of drama books appropriate to each lesson. It is also an invaluable theater resource book. Listed are the names of available play anthologies and theater history books, theater supply houses, film and record sources, and theater organizations and periodicals. As if that were not enough, it also contains a list of play and musical publishers and addresses, as well as an expanded bibliography of theater books for students and teachers. Need I say more?

Looking for more specialized books?

A comprehensive, well-illustrated theater history book appropriate for the high school student is *The Theatre: A Concise History*, by Phyllis Hartnoll. This wonderful book highlights the major periods in theater history and manages not to overwhelm or bore the average student. Beautifully condensed, it comes in paperback at a reasonable price. This book is gold.

If you teach acting, consider Boleslavsky's *Acting: The First Six Lessons*. Although somewhat advanced for freshmen and sophomores, it is a challenging book for upperclassmen. Thought-provoking and insightful, this book provides a good basic introduction to Stanislavski.

For teaching stage makeup, a basic textbook for the adolescent actor is *Simple Makeup for Young Actors*, by Richard Cummings.

When purchasing plays for course study, consider anthologies instead of individual scripts. Not only are they more economical, but they're more durable. They're also more versatile. For example, an anthology of selected plays from various periods in history is a perfect accompaniment to a unit or course in theater history. It can also be used as a text in a general course in dramatic literature or to illustrate the styles and forms of drama in either an acting or creative writing course. Most anthologies come in paperback and are reasonably priced. A current issue of *Paperbound Books in Print*, available in your library as well as at most bookstores, is your best source.

If you have little or no money for play anthologies or scripts for the classroom, there are alternatives. If your courses come under the English department, find out what the department's policy is for outside readings. When students are given a choice of titles for book reports, many schools have a separate budget set up for purchasing these books. In other schools the students are required to buy them. You can assign a specific play as an outside reading, then either order and pay for the plays through this fund, or have students purchase their own scripts. Leaving no stone unturned, speak to the head of the English department. She may have old, soon-to-be-discarded English textbooks sitting in a school storage room that may contain plays suitable for your course.

If your courses come under a drama or a fine arts department and classes are made up of students from the same grade, consider team teaching. Determine which plays are scheduled for study in each grade's English curriculum, then coordinate with the English teachers to teach the same plays. This gives students the opportunity to concentrate on the literary form in one class and to study the production aspect of the same play in the other. It wouldn't be necessary to provide scripts, since students would use an assigned English book in both classes.

Some drama teachers resort to purchasing plays with their own money, or photocopying scripts—which is costly, and above all, *illegal*. A word therefore must be said about the copying of literary works for educational use. To avoid copyright infringement, every teacher should be aware of the laws governing educational photocopying. In his book *The Copyright Book: A Practical Guide*, 3d edition, William S. Strong explains in understandable terms the guidelines established by the Ad Hoc Committee of Educational Institutions and Organizations on Copyright Law Revision, the Authors League of America, Inc., and the Association of American Publishers, Inc. I have provided these guidelines in appendix 5 of this book.

If there's no budgeted money for books and no workable alternative the first year, request funds for the following school year. Justifying your need should be an easy task.

When money is limited for student textbooks, the drama teacher's saving grace is the school's copying machines. Whenever books are unavailable, require students to bring a ring-bound notebook to class and provide them with copies of your prepared lesson material. Use available funds to buy theater reference books.

Among the many books available for compiling lesson material, there are four I would never be without.

The first is Viola Spolin's *Improvisation for the Theater: A Handbook of Teaching and Directing Techniques*, 4th edition. This book of theater games is appropriate for all ages and is ideal for teaching creative dramatics as well as the basics of acting. No drama teacher should be without it.

The second is *Promptbook: A Comprehensive Guide for Teaching Adolescents the Techniques of Acting*, by Bruce Zortman. This book features lesson plans for the basic acting course. Areas covered include improvisation, stage movement, vocal projection, and scene production. Structured to cover a forty-minute class period, each lesson focuses on developing creativity instead of mimicry in young actors. The book also includes reproducible diagrams, exercises, and evaluations.

The third is *TechOne: A Comprehensive Guide for Teaching Adolescents the Skills of Technical Theater*. Another Bruce Zortman book, this one features lesson plans for the basic technical theater course. Included are lessons on scenery and prop design and construction; scenic painting; lighting, costume, and makeup design and implementation; and set model construction techniques.

The fourth is *Respect for Acting*, by Uta Hagen with Haskel Frankel. This book contains a series of acting exercises developed by one of the theater's greatest actors and teachers of acting. This is an invaluable text for helping young actors tackle three-dimensional roles.

If you care to invest your own money, the following state of the art books serve well in any teaching situation, and although pricey, should become part of every drama teacher's personal reference library:

History of the Theatre, 6th edition, by Oscar G. Brockett. An instructor's manual is also available.

Stage Costume Design: Theory, Technique and Style, 2d edition, by Douglas A. Russell.

Scenic Design and Stage Lighting, 6th edition, by W. Oren Parker and Harvey K. Smith.

Stage Makeup, 8th edition, by Richard Corson.

Valuable reference books for play production include:

Here's How: A Basic Stagecraft Book by Herbert V. Hake. Provides a complete and graphic explanation of methods for handling fundamental stagecraft problems. Written in an easy-to-read style every layman can understand.

How to Produce the Play: The Complete Production Handbook by John Wray Young and Margaret Mary Young. An invaluable guide containing easy-to-follow organizational procedures as well as time-tested methods for handling all of the production elements.

Putting on the School Play: A Complete Handbook by Adrienne K. Holtje and Grace A. Mayr. Shows you simple economical ways to build props, costumes, and scenery, and gives pointers for solving nitty gritty production problems. Also details the production process, step by step, from the moment you decide to produce a play to closing night clean-up.

Other books worth noting include:

Stagecraft for Nonprofessionals, 3d edition, by F. A. Buerki.

The Stage Lighting Handbook, 4th edition, by Francis Reid.

Theatre Backstage from A to Z, 3d edition, by Warren C. Lounsbury.

Besides buying books and classroom materials, a drama teacher must also learn how to work with limited funds for mounting public productions. Whether bills are to be paid with budgeted money or money from box office receipts, here are some helpful tips to ease you through production costs and help save money.

Some schools work with approved contractors and require drama teachers to obtain school requisition forms or vouchers for purchases from the administration or department head. However, if your school does not work with approved contractors, begin by setting up charge accounts with local paint and hardware stores, and a local lumber yard, in order to delay payment. Or try to make special arrangements with local suppliers to extend credit until the production goes up. That way expenses can be paid with money taken in from ticket sales and program ads. Keep accurate records of expenditures and hold all receipts. Also record the names of individuals who may buy materials or pay bills with out-of-pocket money so they can be reimbursed at the end of the show's run.

If the school stage lacks essential stage and lighting equipment, it's possible (or probable) that care and upkeep of the auditorium or theater in your school is handled through a general building maintenance fund or through the custodial budget. If it is, try to purchase or replace stage or lighting equipment, including lamps, through one of these budgets instead of your own.

If you need to buy tools for production work, start with essentials. The following list, taken from *How to Produce the Play: The Complete Production Handbook* by John Wray Young and Margaret Mary Young, p. 30, includes the basic tools needed to build the scenery required for most plays:

Crosscut saw	Try square
Ripsaw	Pocket tape
Compass saw	Spirit level
Keyhole saw	Draw knife
Coping saw	Sheep nose pliers
Hack saw	Pipe wrench
Miter saw and miter box	Medium size wrecking bar
Two claw hammers	Push drill
Rip hammer	Wood chisel
One tack hammer	Framing square
Staple gun	Yardsticks
Brace and bit	Plane
Various size screwdrivers	Wood file
Ratchet screwdriver	Monkey wrench
Tin snips	C-clamp

All of these can be purchased at any hardware store for a reasonable price. You might also try thrift stores and garage or tag sales.

Here are a few other money-saving options:

Buy bleached rather than unbleached muslin for covering flats. Not only is it more economical, it is also stronger and requires very little sizing.

Eliminate the use of glue for covering flats. A cleaner and simpler method (shown in appendix 4) saves the cost and mess of a glue pot and will create smooth-surfaced flats unmarred by tack heads, glue "burn-throughs," and the awful odor of glue.

If you plan to purchase power tools, the easiest, least expensive, and relatively safest for students are the electric drill and saber saw. If you plan to buy a circular saw, consider that circular saws require *expert* care and skill in handling. They should only be used by an adult, or at the very least, restricted to use by a limited number of responsible students skilled in their operation *with an adult present.*

Since all power tools are potentially dangerous when not used properly, it's important to know your school's liability policy. Some are more restrictive than others. I taught in one school where the teacher in charge was held personally liable for any student injury. Drama students were forbidden to use electric tools or even to climb ladders to hang and gel lights.

When teaching circumstances make the purchase or use of hand and power tools difficult or impossible, there are other approaches. When feasible, have students working on construction bring in hammers, screwdrivers, hand saws, and other tools from home. Make sure they initial each tool in order to avoid loss and confusion.

Develop a working relationship with your school's industrial arts teachers. If wood needs cutting, arrange for the shop teacher or a shop student to cut it during the school day. Since most schools require teachers to remain in their classrooms a half hour after school in order to be available for students, it may also be possible for drama students to work in the shop during this time under the woodworking teacher's supervision.

Keep in mind, however, that soliciting the help of the industrial arts department requires considerable organization and coordination. You will need to determine well in advance what must be accomplished on any given day. Success in this approach will also depend on the availability of school facilities and the willingness of shop teachers to assist.

Since every drama teacher needs a stock of reusable stage hardware, buy steel stage screws rather than those of malleable iron. They're stronger and will last much longer.

Ask the metals teacher to make stage cleats and other simple stage pieces. In one school I persuaded the metals teacher to weld together metal frames and casters for stage wagons for rolling set pieces on and off the stage. Whatever the shop teachers will make for you will save that much more time and money.

It is therefore to your advantage to develop a working relationship with the industrial arts teachers. Try to impress upon them how essential their help can be. Go out of your way to show your appreciation when they do help. Give them personal recognition in your program or provide complimentary tickets to your production. Remember, a little thanks goes a long way.

The fact remains that some teachers will always be more accommodating than others. So, if for some reason you can't solicit their help, talk to the administration. When you state your needs and your goals clearly and convincingly, the principal may be able to remedy the situation.

Working with a limited budget demands a great deal of creativity and ingenuity. So whenever money is scarce, exercise your options. Learn to maximize available school and community resources, and learn to work with your school's administration and faculty.

7

Maintaining an Active After-School Program

Once a drama curriculum is established, what can a teacher do to maintain an influx of students in school productions? After establishing a production schedule, this is your main goal. There are four basic things a drama teacher can do to maintain an influx of students auditioning and participating in production work and at the same time keep a program running smoothly.

1. Establish an apprenticeship program.

The best way to keep students interested and challenged is to train them in various areas of play production and stagecraft with the intention that they in turn train others. Those who participate in the program from one year to the next should be given more responsibilities. By their senior year, they will have matured and accumulated enough theater experience to enable them, with your guidance, to organize and take charge of younger, less experienced students.

This approach has several benefits. Students are given a unique opportunity to serve as role models; they're provided with invaluable growth and leadership opportunities that will build their confidence and motivate them to do their best. What's more, apprenticeship ensures a steady stream of skilled students and helps maintain your theater program in perpetuity.

2. Instill in students a sense of commitment and responsibility.

From the beginning, adolescents need reinforcement as well as follow-up to stay on track during the production process. When students apply for staff or crew head positions, explain in detail the duties and work requirements. If they accept the responsibilities and produce well, let them know. Even though a job well done may be its own reward, acknowledgement of good work is an even greater bonus. A word of encouragement and appreciation now and then does more to motivate a student than anything else.

If students fail in their commitment, confront them. Make them understand how their lack of responsibility affects everyone's work as well as the production. Once students have been warned, improvement should be immediate; if not, they should be replaced, and told specifically why. Accountability, *especially* at this age, is a must.

Without a doubt some production staff positions are more demanding than others in terms of work and responsibility. While I keep most staff openings available for all productions, students in charge of box office and publicity are required to hold their staff position for the school year. At the end of the year, students are given the option to keep these positions until they graduate. If they choose not to, they are required to train students taking over. This is one of the best ways to maintain continuity and consistency in these two production areas. Students holding these positions are given a chance to develop and maintain consistent record-keeping and bookkeeping systems from one show to the next. The publicity head is also given time to develop and expand a list of businesses for program ads.

However, if you feel you are locking out other students interested in these jobs, or find students in the job losing interest and effectiveness, have students apply for these positions on a production-by-production basis. While the frequent retraining required in this approach might prove less convenient than having a "permanent" person in the job, it does have the benefit of giving more students the opportunity to hold these positions and of giving you a larger pool of qualified students to choose from if someone gets sick or drops out and needs to be replaced. Both approaches have advantages and disadvantages worth considering.

When students know where you stand and what is expected, they learn quickly the importance of commitment and responsibility in play production. More importantly, they learn how essential each individual is to a company, which in many cases is enough incentive to keep them in the program.

3. Involve as many departments as you can.

Assistance from the home economics, vocational, art, and music departments eases the production burden and enhances the quality of your program. The joint effort boosts morale. It improves teacher/student relationships and creates better school spirit.

4. Develop a working relationship with your school's custodians.

These individuals are *indispensable* to the drama teacher. As managers of the school building, they literally open doors. In addition to their making after-school and evening rehearsals possible, they have access to locked classrooms, tools, ladders, light bulbs, brooms, buckets, and other indispensable basics.

Furthermore, administration permission to conduct certain activities or use certain facilities does not always guarantee that you'll have free access to those facilities. The school atmosphere changes drastically after school hours. For the most part, it's only you and the custodians, and no one else. They can make things easy or difficult, so learn to work with them. They're also the only school personnel you can turn to when emergencies arise during after-school or evening rehearsals. By this time, the school administration and faculty are long gone. Who else can give you that desperately needed half hour to complete a dress or tech rehearsal before the school is locked up for the night? You guessed it.

Developing a rapport with your school custodians is important. Never take them for granted. When you show how much you appreciate their help, chances are you'll find them not only accommodating, but also a refreshing change from the school's hierarchy and bureaucracy. They're often the friendliest, most down-to-earth employees in the school system.

Part III

THE ADOLESCENT

It takes courage to grow up and turn out to be who you really are.

—e.e. cummings

THE AGE OF PREDICTABILITY

Teaching drama at the secondary level can be richly reward-ing. You will experience fewer problems when you under-stand the adolescent and learn what to expect and how to respond. But what is it that motivates their thinking and their behavior? They're not as complicated as they may seem at first, and once you begin teaching, you'll quickly discover how predictable they can be.

Although each child is unique, all adolescent problems and challenges are fundamentally the same. Adolescents are children in transition experiencing intense emotional and physiological changes that often leave them feeling awkward, frustrated, and confused. These changes can dramatically affect mood, as well as attitude and performance. Wants and desires are in direct conflict with doubts and fears. They want their independence, yet are still in constant need of guidance; they want to be understood when they hardly understand themselves.

Adolescents also need social acceptance and to be part of a group, for they lack the self-confidence to function alone. Their lives are becoming increasingly complicated. Everyday problems that may seem trivial to an adult can be devastating and seemingly insurmountable to an adolescent.

Yet as complex as adolescents appear to be, they all share the same basic needs. They need constant encouragement. They need to learn that one grows from mistakes and that success in anything comes from persevering and accepting responsibility. They need to laugh at themselves and be more tolerant of others. They also need to learn that self-love leads to self-respect as well as respect for others. They need to learn to trust their instincts and be true to themselves by never allowing others to define who they are, or what they can be. And above all, they need to know someone cares.

As difficult as adolescents can be, they possess unique qualities. They have limitless potential. They're perceptive, quick, and open to new ideas and challenges. They're extremely observant and creative, as well as ingenious when the need arises. Once motivated, they'll work as hard as you're willing to push them. And once they've put their mind to something, they'll keep on trying when many adults would have given up.

A large part of secondary school teaching involves coping with the moods and attitudes of adolescents. As your students grow and change, so must your teaching approach. Each grade has its own specific problems, just as each age has its typical behavioral patterns. You'll need to know what these basic characteristics are, and what you as a drama teacher should do, as well as avoid, to make theater a positive experience at every grade level.

8

Working with the
Adolescent Actor

The most difficult and intense period of adolescent growth occurs in grades seven through nine. These are challenging grades to teach, for the onset of puberty dramatically affects how students relate to teachers and how they interact with peers in the classroom. Understanding these changes and how they affect student attitudes, particularly in the drama situation, will help you deal with this age group more effectively. It will also help you determine the right teaching approach to use during each stage of growth.

Keep in mind, however, that the rate of emotional growth and physical development of students between ages twelve and fifteen varies greatly. It also varies in students of the *same* age. As a result, no two adolescents in this age bracket respond to drama in the same way. Also keep in mind that the following behavioral patterns may occur in an earlier or later grade. Let's examine the general attitudes and behavioral patterns of each age, and the grades where they're *most likely* to occur. Included are recommended teaching methods and approaches.

THE SEVENTH-GRADE STUDENT:
Age of Fleeting Childhood

Seventh grade students are usually twelve to thirteen years old. For the most part, both boys and girls are within the same range of maturity. In the initial stages of puberty, young adolescents still possess the spark of uninhibitedness and the spontaneity of childhood. Their shyness is more the result of apprehension in a new situation than of self-consciousness, and usually disappears once they're comfortable with a teacher. The growth spurts that begin around age twelve often lead to problems in coordination and account for much of the physical awkwardness and clumsiness of adolescence.

Early adolescents need physical activity to release bottled-up energy, and therefore should not be inactive in the class-room for more than fifteen minutes, after which all concentration is gone. Girls are more socially oriented and find release by gathering in groups and gabbing. Boys are more physically oriented and find their release through a more aggressive behavior. When forced to sit passively for too long they often feel compelled to push, kick, or punch someone.

As drama students, twelve- to thirteen-year-olds respond best to classes where they are actively engaged and where verbal feedback is forthcoming. They are best motivated in an activity-oriented class where a dynamic teaching approach is used. Because the joy of play is not yet lost, this age group is receptive to all theater games and exercises. As actors, they are highly imaginative and creative in skits and pantomimes. Play production, however, is where they find the most enjoyment.

Producing a class play not only exposes them to production elements, but also serves as a perfect vehicle for introducing other aspects of theater. For example, try using a period play to teach a specific period in theater history. Present a play's historical background in story form using pictures and slides; bring in period costumes for students to examine or model; do a makeup demonstration of one of the play's characters. Remember, students at this stage of growth learn best through a visual, hands-on teaching approach. No matter what aspect of theater you teach, incorporate activities and demonstrations into each lesson. Activities that stimulate reaction and participation from the class are always effective.

Avoid straight lecturing. Thirteen-year-olds are poor note-takers. Not only is this activity too passive, but early adolescents also suffer a temporary loss of legibility in writing caused more by changing biology than carelessness. If the material being covered is lengthy or difficult for students to grasp quickly, distribute mimeographed information or worksheets to be completed during class. In short, involve students in lessons by keeping subject matter basic and relevant. Look for verbal feedback, and make use of demonstrations and props whenever possible. If this high-energy group is not kept active, boredom will quickly become restlessness—which often leads to problems in discipline.

In terms of student interaction, the most difficult problem for seventh-graders is working with the opposite sex. With puberty occurring at an earlier age, today's twelve- to thirteen-year-olds are beginning to test the waters sooner than ever before; many are already dating. However, they are often awkward and shy when forced into close interaction in the *classroom* setting. If you ask a group of boys and girls of this age to form a circle for a theater game, nine times out of ten you'll end up with two half circles, girls on one side, boys on the other, with a two-foot space separating the two. At this age, rarely will members of the opposite sex pair up voluntarily for theater exercises, making relating one to one an even more difficult problem.

The best solution: don't make it an issue. When girls and boys must work together, have the class choose a partner by drawing names from a hat, or pair them up yourself. In this way selection is handled fairly and feelings are never hurt. Also avoid contact games where there is resistance to touching or holding hands. Forcing physical contact will only make students uncomfortable and less willing to participate. These are sensitive issues at this age, so never make light of them.

The key to working effectively with seventh-graders is to make drama a form of organized recreation. Channel student energies into theater activities that stimulate imagination, spontaneity, and above all, active participation.

THE EIGHTH-GRADE STUDENT:
Age of Contradiction

Eighth grade is a completely different experience. In my opinion, fourteen-year-olds are one of the most challenging age groups to teach. Because of the intense emotional and physiological changes taking place, their needs and attitudes are dramatically different from those of the thirteen-year-old.

Adolescents at the height of puberty enter into an intense stage of egocentrism and self-absorption. They are the center of the universe, seeing themselves as indestructible, invincible, and immortal. Living only in the present, they are blind to the consequences of their actions. They are consistently inconsistent, and will contradict simply for the sake of contradiction. They'll love you one day, despise you the next. Unstructured, they will often find it difficult or impossible to follow through on instructions or commitments.

They mostly resent being treated like children. But in spite of attempts to assert themselves, they are controlled by peer pressure more now than ever before. The intense physical changes taking place make them extremely self-conscious and insecure; they dislike being singled out for fear of embarrassment. They will avoid looking or acting differently at all cost, for their sole preoccupation—both in and out of the classroom—is to avoid ridicule and gain the approval and acceptance of their peers.

These changes in attitude are greatly inhibiting, for as

actors, fourteen-year-olds are no longer as spontaneous and imaginative as they were a year ago. They fear looking awkward or clumsy, and are more guarded in their willingness to perform. They would rather be told what to do than initiate anything for fear of looking foolish. The problems resulting from this extreme self-consciousness are compounded by their poor concentration and erratic attention span.

Since creative play is perceived as "childish and stupid" at this stage of development, students need to be told the exact purpose of every theater game and exercise. Paralyzed by acute self-consciousness, they often need specific instructions about what they should do, especially for pantomimes, improvisations, and acting scenes.

The interaction problems of boys and girls at the height of puberty are unique; they're physically and emotionally out of phase. And because girls are more mature than boys, each exhibit different attitudes and patterns of behavior. At their worst, girls are more temperamental and prone to cattiness when provoked. Self-absorbed and mentally preoccupied to distraction, they're usually obsessed with their physical appearance and have a constant need to impress. More socially outgoing, they tend to prefer the company of older boys, finding those their own age extremely boring and uninteresting.

Boys, on the other hand, are more socially introverted. Although some may experience raging hormones and become sexually active sooner than others, they still lag behind girls in emotional and physical maturity. Finding it difficult to prove their masculinity through physical appearance, they often revert to obnoxious behavior in order to impress the opposite sex. Showing off, swearing, or using crude language is common at this age. (See James P. Garvin's *Learning How to Kiss a Frog: Advice for Those Working with Pre- and*

Early Adolescents, p. 17; Mr. Garvin provides further insight into pre- and early adolescent behavior, and also offers invaluable coping skills and teaching strategies.) Confused and struggling with their self-image, boys attempt to assert their masculinity by identifying with typical male activities. Drawn more to competitive sports and vocational subjects, they perceive theater, more often than not, as a subject for *sissies*. The difficulty in teaching boys of this age is to change this perception.

The most effective approach? Teach theater as a discipline and a craft. Expose fourteen-year-old boys as well as girls to the more practical, technical aspects of theater. This includes related stage, acting, and production terminology, as well as the duties and responsibilities of the production staff. Since adolescents of this age begin to acquire higher-level reasoning skills, set up a problem-centered curriculum in which conclusions must be reached.

To stimulate this creative thinking, encourage open-ended class discussions where it is unnecessary to come up with "right answers." Require eighth-graders to take brief notes, and supplement lectures with audio and visual aids in order to provide concrete examples of everything you teach. In addition, provide theater worksheets that students complete during class and use later for study and prepping for quizzes. No matter what aspect of theater you teach, ask questions requiring elaborate responses, thus forcing students to defend their answers. Challenge them with various types of hands-on projects, such as designing and building box set models, building props, writing original skits—anything that requires discipline, problem solving, precision workmanship, and original thinking.

Adolescents at this growth stage need to begin making decisions and accepting more responsibility to boost their self-image. Ego support is crucial at this age (Garvin, p. 24).

When producing a class play, require that they handle all production details and give them the opportunity to accept the responsibilities of authority. Organize a production staff and hand them the reins.

My selection process is simple. I begin by explaining the duties and responsibilities of each staff position, then fill these positions by drawing names of interested students from a hat. Once they're filled, remaining students are required to sign up and serve in a production crew. Giving students choices and specific duties helps them understand how essential the production organization is to the play, and also promotes positive interaction and cooperation within the class.

Caught emotionally between adolescence and childhood, students at this stage of development have unique acting and interaction problems that warrant special attention. A drama teacher should therefore build a drama course around more structured, disciplined theater activities that encourage cooperation and stimulate creative thinking. This will help students develop self-control, a better sense of self, and a greater sense of responsibility.

THE NINTH-GRADE STUDENT:
Age of Adjustment

Ninth-graders undergo a major period of adjustment because their behavior and attitudes are affected by a larger scope of influences. Although most school systems have four-year high schools, some still subscribe to the junior high structure of grades seven through nine. The behavior of junior high ninth-graders is markedly different than that of high school freshmen. Being the oldest and serving as role models for the younger students, they tend to exhibit more self-confidence and a greater sense of responsibility. However, because their high school entry is delayed a year, they find themselves isolated socially and experience frustration and resentment because of it. Simply put—*they don't want to be there.* Too old to associate with seventh- and eighth-graders, they hunger for the high school experience; after the last period bell, they are likely to run to the high school to meet with friends and participate in after-school activities. This social displacement and developmental delay are why many school systems are abandoning the junior high framework in favor of the middle school structure of grades six through eight.

High school freshmen, on the other hand, are struggling through major adjustments. From the fifteen-year-old's perspective, leaving the protective, closely supervised years of middle school for the more demanding, decision-making years of high school can be both exhilarating and overwhelming. Interaction with older high school students alone creates new social pressures and expectations.

There are also increased academic demands. With more challenges and responsibilities thrust upon them, ninth-graders need more than emotional support; they need vocational guidance as well. All these factors make adjustment much more difficult.

As a group, fifteen-year-olds have weathered through the most volatile period of puberty. The discipline problems associated with early adolescence become less intrusive in the high school classroom. The childlike, disruptive behavior found in junior high has all but disappeared. In addition, fifteen-year-olds begin to lose their need for group attachments and move towards developing personal relationships. Although the maturity gap between boys and girls of this age is closing, girls are still ahead by at least a year.

As actors, fifteen-year-olds are timid and cautious in performance situations, but compared to fourteen-year-olds, they are less inhibited and less critical of one another. They are more mature, self-controlled, and for the most part, more responsible as students. They do, however, need to develop concrete reasoning skills and therefore must be challenged intellectually. Show them how to assimilate information—to see parts and how they are related to the whole—for this leads to upper-level thinking skills.

Whether teaching middle school, junior or senior high, it's also important that you teach all facets of theater, including abstract concepts and theories in concrete terms. Until adolescents are ready to conceptualize, you must continue to introduce drama material in a way that will make sense to them, namely, through visual and kinesthetic activities and tasks. These practical approaches are key to developing drama as a serious academic subject on the secondary level.

Around age sixteen, age and maturity differences are recognized less through behavior, and more through attitude and the quality of academic performance. The main concern of the drama teacher is deciding the amount, depth, and scope of course material that will best challenge the student.

THE HIGH SCHOOL STUDENT:
Age of Self-Assertion

Without a doubt high school is one of the most impressionable periods of adolescent life. Once initial adjustments in ninth or tenth grade have been made, students undergo extraordinary changes. Fifteen- and sixteen-year-olds exhibit a youthful exuberance and enthusiasm in classes and in school activities; they fully immerse themselves in day-to-day events. The high school experience becomes for them a time for self-assertion, and for challenging and questioning everything; a time for testing and exploring anything new as well as outrageous, often to the consternation of parents and teachers. Although peer pressure still remains a constant in their lives, ninth- and tenth-graders are discovering who they are.

With increasing maturity, seventeen- and eighteen-year-olds become more introspective as they begin to define their values and beliefs, and find direction in their lives. Struggling through this last phase of adolescence into young adulthood, juniors and seniors think more about the future, and begin to explore life's possibilities.

Emotionally, these students are in a constant flux. At times, their optimism, energy, and enthusiasm seem inexhaustible. They have the unique ability to accomplish anything presented to them through sheer force of will. Yet their failures, disappointments, and fears often devastate and paralyze them. Although every school has its share of overachievers, the typical, average teenager will do things the hard way because he doesn't think problems through. At his worst, he will often try to get by with doing nothing.

High school drama students in general need to be pushed and challenged creatively. Original ideas don't come easily. As actors, they tend to portray characters in stereotypical terms. Internalizing a role at this age is difficult, for they have trouble getting in touch with feelings and expressing emotions, and have little life experience to draw from.

A drama teacher must understand the underlying problems that stifle creativity and hinder acting ability at this age, as well as understand how to draw out talent and get the best performances from students.

9

Basic Acting Problems
and Solutions

For many years I depended solely on the basic techniques of Stanislavski and Boleslavsky to teach acting. But I often found these approaches difficult for the secondary level acting student to fully grasp. Asking adolescents to analyze and probe deeply into their feelings and experiences often became not only counterproductive, but inappropriate and ineffectual in developing acting roles. I felt there had to be a better way to tap into the adolescent's inner resources.

Stanislavski, the great master himself, although viewed as a legendary philosopher who envisioned a mystic method of acting, was first and foremost a practical teacher who continually experimented with his own actors. Once asked about The Method, he replied: "Create your *own* method. Don't depend slavishly on mine. Make up something that will work for you!" (Moore, *The Stanislavski System*, p. xv).

Well, experiment I did, and finally found a simpler, more direct approach that produced results when all else failed. The technique I use is closely tied to a science called Neuro-Linguistic Programming (NLP).

NLP is the study of how language, both verbal and nonverbal, affects the nervous system. The theory is that the ability to accomplish anything in life is based upon one's ability to use the brain in an optimal way. People who produce outstanding results do so by producing specific communications to and through the nervous system. NLP, therefore, provides a systematic framework for directing the brain. It teaches how to direct not only our own states and behaviors, but also those of others. (See Anthony Robbins's *Unlimited Power*, p. 26; Mr. Robbins explains in great detail the principles of NLP and their practical application.)

One of the major precepts of NLP affirms that a person's attitudes and emotional states are reflected in his physiology. As an example, lack of confidence, fear, and depression, as well as assertiveness, confidence, and joy automatically induce a correlating response in body stance, and in head, shoulder, and eye position. If you change the state of mind, body posture will automatically change; and conversely, if you change body posture, the state of mind will change. Mind and body are inextricably linked. Our internal representation and physiology work together in a cybernetic loop; change one, and you instantly change the other (Robbins, p. 150). Applying these cybernetic principles to training the adolescent actor can produce astounding results in a short time.

One of the major obstacles young actors need to overcome is self-consciousness and nervousness. In adolescents, this problem is often exacerbated by poor body image. Teenagers are fraught with anxiety over how they look. Having pimples, being too short or too tall, too skinny or too fat makes them even more insecure. Helping adolescents overcome "performance anxiety" greatly depends on bolstering their confidence. To do this, a drama teacher must first change how students perceive themselves by putting them in a more resourceful, empowering frame of mind. Since self-consciousness and nervousness are uncomfortable stressful states, it is necessary to change these internal representations to more desirable and comfortable ones.

When a student feels self-conscious or nervous, simply ask her to *look* confident and relaxed on stage, whether she believes she is or not. When a student *pretends* to be confident, she adopts the posture of a person who is confident. In no time she begins to *feel* confident and relaxed, for the act alone triggers the corresponding mental state. When you consistently induce this confident attitude and posture in students, you will not only see their performance dramatically improve, you will also see them interact with others more effectively in theater exercises and games.

This "acting as if" exercise is also effective in solving basic acting problems. Let's say an actor has trouble staying in character. I will say to him, "Act as if you were concentrating. Stand the way you would stand if you *were* this character. Breathe the way you'd be breathing if you were this character *right now*. Make your face look as if you were in character *at this very moment*." As soon as the student stands and breathes the way I ask and uses his physiology to reflect the proper state, he is instantly in character. This approach works because it focuses the actor by sharpening his concentration and enhances his self-image by increasing his confidence.

Teaching students how to control and change their physiology at will in this way ultimately helps them access the proper state of mind for scene and character work. But any skill requires practice. The best way for you to help your students gain better control over breathing, posture, facial expressions, and the overall quality of movement is to continually expose them to exercises and activities that increase body awareness.

Directing young actors to change their physiology also helps them do things they could never do before, because the moment a change in physiology occurs, a change in state of mind occurs as well. You can use this technique when an actor has difficulty getting in touch with emotions for a role. Have the student verbalize and concentrate on the emotion called for in the scene by stating the emotion required, such as "I am . . . angry, sad, happy, etc." Have her repeat it over and over until her physiology changes.

For example, ask a student to repeat "I am powerful" several times. As she repeats the statement, you will see her instantly transformed: her head, eyes, and chest will begin to rise, her muscles will relax, and her breathing will slow. In a matter of seconds, she will become a picture of poise and confidence.

Next ask the same student to repeat and focus fully on the phrase "I am afraid." In no time, the chest will begin to sink, the arms and hands will fidget, and the eyes and head will lower. All of this will occur without conscious "emotional recall." When the student verbalizes and repeats the emotion, she will begin to *feel* the emotion *and* its physical effects as well.

Verbalizing emotions is especially effective in scene work. When actors have trouble creating well-motivated characters, I require them to discover and state the core or underlying emotion or feeling that drives each character in a scene. Students are then asked to improvise the scene through that emotion. Again, repeating the emotion will immediately affect the posture, breathing patterns, muscle tension, and tonality of the actors and quickly focus them on their purpose and motivation in the scene.

To try out this technique with your students, pair up actors and have them memorize the short scene below:

1st Actor: Let's get out of here.

2nd Actor: I'm busy.

1st Actor: Forget about that.

2nd Actor: I can't.

1st Actor: Maybe this will change your mind.

2nd Actor: Oh, boy.

1st Actor: We're wasting precious time.

2nd Actor: I know.

Next, have actors play out the scene using a scenario of their own, or using the scenarios below. (Props and furniture may be used.)

Scenario #1: The Lottery Winner
Underlying emotions: euphoria and impatience
(*1st Actor:* I'm ecstatic. *2nd Actor:* I'm annoyed.)

Scenario #2: The Double Agent Double-cross
Underlying emotions: anxiety and courage
(*1st Actor:* I'm nervous. *2nd Actor:* I'm confident.)

Scenario #3: The Hostage
Underlying emotions: rage and defiance
(*1st Actor:* I'm furious. *2nd Actor:* I'm daring.)

Scenario #4: The Blackmail Note
Underlying emotions: panic and sorrow
(*1st Actor:* I'm terrified. *2nd Actor:* I'm miserable.)

Scenario #5: Cupid Strikes
Underlying emotions: infatuation and hostility
(*1st Actor:* I'm lovesick. *2nd Actor:* I'm combative.)

By concentrating on the stated emotions, young actors are able to create a believable scene. In playing out each scenario, the different emotions suggested (or any others that may surface) will focus them on the acting endeavor as well as the action and business required to make the scene work.

Remember, emotions are what propel us to action. Whether young or old, everyone experiences them in the same way, regardless of the circumstances that created the emotional state. (I am referring here to how emotions feel and manifest themselves physically in the body, not to how they're acted out.) Grief, whether caused by the loss of a cherished pet or a cherished loved one, creates the same pain. Grief is grief, regardless of cause or intensity. Fear is fear. Anger is anger.

Physicalizing emotions through the use of stage props or stage business will *reinforce* emotion, but the emotion alone will lead the actor to his motivation and purpose in a scene. Get an actor to isolate the emotion, focus only on that emotion, and experience how the body responds to that emotion, and he can fit that emotion into the context of any scene.

Another presupposition of NLP is that all humans share the same neurology. You can therefore do anything someone else can do if you operate your nervous system in a like manner. This process of copying exactly what others do to produce a specific result is commonly referred to as modeling (Robbins, p. 27). If you want to become rich, model the steps and approaches of a Henry Ford or a John D. Rockefeller. If you wish to become a better athlete, model the training of an Olympic gold medalist.

On that basis, modeling is an effective visualization technique in helping young actors find direction in a role, especially since the adolescent has little life experience to draw upon. Modeling famous actors or familiar people helps young actors trigger desired emotions, and grasp the attitudes and intent of a character more quickly.

This type of imaging is particularly effective in staging group scenes and choreographing production numbers. For example, to stage the ballroom scene for a production of *My Fair Lady*, I used this technique not only to teach students to waltz, but also to create an atmosphere of elegance, regality, and sophistication in the scene.

The first step was to put students in the proper frame of mind. I started with posture. Students were to assume the stance of trained dancers and were not allowed to slouch or ramble during dance rehearsals. Since my students were familiar with the classic dance duo of Astaire and Rogers, I reinforced this behavior by having each boy picture himself as

Fred Astaire, and each girl as Ginger Rogers. By using the "acting as if" approach and modeling technique, I immediately put them in a confidence mode. This made it easier for them to learn to waltz and also motivated them to practice and perfect each move.

In no time, this small group of students who once believed themselves incapable of dancing a single step were transformed from awkward, uncoordinated teenagers into poised, elegant, sophisticated upper crust aristocrats on stage. By changing their physiology through visualization and modeling, I was able to instill in them a positive attitude about learning to dance. Using these two techniques also improved their concentration and induced the appropriate state of mind to create a believable scene.

The "acting as if" approach and modeling techniques were used effectively to create an atmosphere of elegance and sophistication in this high school production of "My Fair Lady."

Teaching young actors to verbalize and physicalize attitudes and feelings not only helps them overcome self-consciousness, shyness, and the fear of performing, it is also an effective way to help them experience and express the emotions needed to create believable characters.

To make students aware of the subtle psychological components of a character, consider using this two-part exercise. Have students re-create on stage two ordinary minutes of their life, presenting it as though it were happening for the first time. (See Uta Hagen and Haskel Frankel's *Respect for Acting*, p. 82.) The first part of the exercise requires a written homework assignment. When students are alone performing a simple task, they are to observe and make note of everything in their immediate environment. The activity can be as simple as writing a letter, watching TV, doing homework, getting something to eat, etc. In recording this undertaking, they must answer the following questions.

QUESTION	EXAMPLE OF ANSWER
Who am I? (The student as the character)	I'm a high school senior; president of the drama club; son of two workaholic parents; a lousy mathematician; a James Dean fan; a human being who loves acting, girls, thrills, and my trusty Harley-Davidson.
What am I doing? (Activity)	I'm studying for a calculus exam.
What time is it? (Year, season, day, minute, atmosphere)	7:30 P.M. on Tuesday, November 3, 1992. The presidential election results are coming in on the evening news. It's windy outside. The air is cool, but not cold enough to turn on the heat. I'm wearing a turtleneck sweater to keep warm.

Where am I?
(City, neighborhood, house, room, area of room)

My house is on Hill Road in Barnard. I'm sitting at an oak desk in my room. There is a window behind my desk. I can see the Zimmermans' well-lit gray shingled house through the bare branches of the maple tree that separates our property.

What surrounds me?
(People, animate and inanimate objects)

There is an opened calculus book and a large scratch pad in front of me. Several notebooks stuffed with school papers are to my right, and a computer sits on a small table to my left. An oak wall unit to my right houses a stereo, CD and cassette tapes, two old pony league trophies, an assortment of books, and a portable TV. There's an old wicker chair in the corner behind me filled with dirty laundry and a gym bag. My bed sits diagonally in the opposite corner. There are two large black and white posters—one of James Dean and another of Charlie Chaplin—hanging on the wall above a night table stacked with *Hot Rod* magazines. My gray cat Bugzy is curled up on my bed pillow directly under a lighted brass wall lamp. I can hear the TV and my parents talking in the den across the hall.

What are the given circumstances?
(Past, present, and future, as well as the events surrounding the activity)

I'm expecting my friend Steve. He's been tutoring me for a few weeks now. I'm barely passing calculus and I need this course for college. Instead of studying when I got home from school, I raked the leaves in the back yard, and cleaned and polished my motorcycle.

What is my relationship? (Relation to total events, pertinent characters and things)	To the calculus course: It's an important factor in my getting accepted into college. To Steve: We've been friends since grammar school. He's a math whiz and I'm depending on him to help pull me through this course.
What do I want? (Major life goals, main and immediate objectives)	*Life goals:* I want to be rich and successful, and to travel the world. *Main objective:* To pass this calculus exam. *Immediate objective:* To finish these math problems before Steve gets here.
What's in my way? (Obstacles)	*Time:* Steve will be here in half an hour. I'm having trouble concentrating; if I flunk and end up on the ineligible list, I'll have to give up the lead in the school play. *Other homework:* I have an English paper due tomorrow. *Attitude:* I'd rather be doing anything else but sitting here. My mechanical pencil is out of lead and I can't find an extra lead anywhere. I've misplaced my eraser and I keep losing my place in the book.
What do I do to get what I want?	I shut the door to my room. I find another pencil. I hold the book open with a paperweight. I focus on the problems, write out the math formulas, and work each problem through to the end.

Once students have determined all of the physical, emotional, and psychological components surrounding their chosen activity, they'll be ready to outline the action for a two-minute scene and perform it in class. By having young actors re-create a scene from their own lives, they are able to better understand that the motives and influencing factors that affect them daily are the same elements required to create believable characters on stage.

There are of course no hard-and-fast rules for training young actors. It doesn't matter what technique or approach you use. What matters is that the technique and approach you use *works*. A drama teacher must continually experiment and develop techniques and approaches that get results, for training young actors is an art requiring practice and skill.

10

Selecting Plays for Performance

Selecting plays for the secondary level is, in many ways, also an art. There are many different factors to consider before choosing a play. As previously discussed, the dramatic emotional and physical changes adolescents undergo create specific problems and needs that have to be addressed. It should be no surprise that these changes will affect their taste in play material. Certain types of plays appeal more to one age group than another.

For the most part, students twelve to thirteen years of age enjoy plays with colorful two-dimensional characters and lots of stage action. They are still young enough to enjoy fantasy and adventure plays, as well as plays for holidays and special occasions. By age fourteen, however, most adolescents consider fantasy and adventure "juvenile." They're more comfortable portraying "real," adult-like characters that enhance their changing self-image. They prefer mysteries, melodramas, situational comedies, futuristic plays, and problem plays dealing with teenage life. Around age sixteen, adolescents are mature enough to begin tackling adult roles in every genre. They have also reached the age where they can be comfortable performing children's theater. The one genre, however, that appeals to adolescents of all ages is the musical.

Idea or concept plays such as allegorical and Japanese Nō plays, often seem appropriate for the secondary level because they're easy to stage and have minimal production requirements. Their simplicity makes them even more tempting for the junior high level. But be careful; their symbolic overtones require a level of understanding often beyond the grasp of most adolescents—especially those between thirteen and fourteen, as one student teacher of mine discovered.

This enthusiastic and talented young man persuaded me against my better judgment to let him produce an adaptation of a Nō drama using that year's best eighth grade drama class. He was convinced the play's simple staging would give him time to expose the class to the Eastern philosophy and culture behind the play.

What a mistake.

After several weeks of rehearsals, this bright, well-disciplined class of students turned into a belligerent, out-of-control group of brats. So frustrated by the play's abstract concepts and slow pacing, they reached a breaking point: They threw their scripts at their teacher and refused to rehearse.

The best way to avoid this kind of nightmare? Simple. Make sure a play's theme and subject matter are appropriate for the maturity level of your students and within their capacity to understand and appreciate. (This resilient young man, by the way, did manage to redeem himself. He developed into an excellent teacher and was eventually well liked by his students—it was only the *play* they hated. Later when class attitudes returned to normal and students were justly disciplined, he shelved the Nō drama and produced an action-packed melodrama with great success.)

If you're looking for more intellectually and emotionally challenging plays, you can select from a growing body of dramatic works targeted for the junior high age group, usually referred to as *youtheater* or *theater for youth*. Plays that fall under this category carry mature themes appropriate for students twelve to fifteen years of age. Many successfully

Children's theater productions not only have broad appeal, but are also excellent vehicles for stretching young actors. In this montage of scenes from "Alice in Wonderland," a story already familiar to many children, the strong characters, simple and effective costumes and props, and inventive casting—a boy as the Duchess!— add up to a memorable show.

intertwine fantasy and realism and deal effectively with such topics as aging, death and dying, courage, conformity, prejudice, maturation, sexuality, and divorce, as well as struggles with moral judgments. (A listing of plays with mature themes geared to this age group is included in appendix 6.)

Whether teaching junior or senior high, consider carefully the time a play is to be produced. Will it be rehearsed and performed *during* school hours as part of an activity-oriented drama class, or *after* school as an extracurricular activity?

When selecting plays for after-school activities, you have freedom to pick almost any play. The show can be cast from a large selection of students, and as much rehearsal time can be scheduled as needed. On the other hand, in-class productions are more restricting. You must choose plays with enough parts to match the number of students in a class and work with whatever talent your students have. You must also cope with the problem of limited rehearsal time.

One solution is to find a play that can be rehearsed from beginning to end during one school period. In this way all class members can participate in each day's rehearsals. You will have more consistency in daily routine, better control over class activities, and fewer problems with discipline.

If a play takes more than a class period to rehearse, be sure the students not scheduled for rehearsal have something to do. Assign in-class projects or work assignments requiring originality and creativity. Or put these students in charge of production details, such as setting up and striking props and sets, prompting lines, and running curtain. You'll spend less time micromanaging and more time rehearsing.

But remember, successful management of a class with different groups of students engaged in different activities *demands* detailed preparations and established classroom procedures, including a consistent routine for rotating production duties and responsibilities. It also requires a classroom or work area large enough to accommodate several group activities at once.

Ultimately, the better solution is to keep in-class productions on a small scale. Look for publishing companies or periodicals offering workshop pieces, or one-act plays specifically geared to the junior and senior high level. The Boston monthly *Plays, The Drama Magazine for Young People*, for example, offers an array of non-royalty plays fifteen to forty-five minutes in length that are simple to produce and easily adapted or expanded for large classes.

When choosing a play for public production, first consider your goals.

Is your primary interest to stretch your actors? To involve as many students as possible? Or to draw a large audience? For a public production to be a success, have all three of these goals in mind.

What type of play is appropriate? The play selected should be well written and have good literary value as well as a worthwhile theme. It should also challenge the creative and artistic abilities of your students. However, a teacher must carefully weigh the potential reaction of the administration and community to plays of literary merit that may contain excessive profanity, objectionable subject matter, or require a sordid and unwholesome presentation of characters. What is considered appropriate in one community may be inappropriate or offensive in another. Drama teachers therefore must keep in mind the cultural makeup, values, and tastes of the community when selecting a play for public performance. Fortunately, there is now available a growing body of quality plays for teens featuring contemporary issue-oriented works that both challenge young actors and generate a positive audience response. (A list of recommended plays for high school is provided in appendix 7.)

If you're thinking about producing one of the great

dramas in order to stretch your actors, consider carefully the aesthetic and artistic demands of the script. Consider carefully whether students are equipped to handle highly sophisticated or advanced roles. Ask yourself: Do my students have the maturity and talent to do *justice* to a serious play? Are they capable of handling the emotional and psychological aspects of a role *well enough* to create believable, three-dimensional characters?

If so, by all means produce them, and produce them often. But remember, junior and senior high school students cannot bring to a role more than they are capable of giving, so be *realistic* in your performance expectations.

Although it's important to challenge your students, it is also important to have an audience to play to. Remember, major productions largely depend on school and community support for funding. Although the classics and great modern dramas are wonderful vehicles for broadening young actors, the fact is, they have limited box office appeal. Unfortunately, they're rarely done well enough at this level to attract the serious theatergoer.

Comedies, melodramas, and musicals, on the other hand, are not only good vehicles for junior and senior high students, they are also good theater. They offer your students the opportunity to perform at their best, and provide good entertainment for the audience. Many plays require large casts, and large cast shows will usually attract a larger, more diversified audience. So if the financial success of a public production is *critical*, select a play that has broad appeal to the school and the community in which you teach.

You can select and purchase both royalty and non-royalty plays from play catalogues that are available through a number of publishers (a directory is included in appendix 8). Some publishers sell preview packages of a sampling of their plays to assist you in your selection. All play catalogues

Comedy classics, like George F. Kaufman's "The Man Who Came to Dinner," offer many challenging roles for high school actors—meaning larger casts with more parts, and consequently, greater student involvement and ticket sales!

provide the price of scripts and royalties, and ordering instructions. When two quotations for royalties are given (for example, *Royalty $50–35*), the first amount quoted is for the first performance, and the second for each subsequent performance. Royalty plays are protected by very stringent copyright laws. Any play that is acted or read on stage before an audience is subject to a royalty fee; and royalties are due on each performance whether or not admission is charged. When presenting scenes from a play or an abbreviated version of a dramatic work, keep in mind that a number of playwrights forbid cuttings of their work, while others allow cuttings only when a full act of their play is performed; revisions, deletions, or piecing together of scenes are forbidden. To perform a cutting of any royalty play, you must apply and receive permission *in writing*.

Most publishers provide perusal copies, scores or demo tapes of musicals either free of charge or for a small fee; the review period may vary from ten days to four weeks. Other publishers sell preview packages made up of selected titles and music demo tapes. Musical royalties are quoted in writing and are based on the number of performances, the expected size of your house, i.e. the number of seats you plan to fill, the price of admission, and whether you require an orchestration. Unless stated differently in the catalogue, royalties are due one week in advance of the first performance.

Part IV

TEACHING BASICS

In order to rule, you must learn how to serve.
—An Ancient Oracle

11

Understanding the Public School Environment

We now come to the "nuts and bolts" of public school teaching. What do you do when you face a class for the first time? What are some common teaching and production problems a drama teacher is most likely to encounter? The remaining part of this book is dedicated to answering these questions. We'll focus on specific classroom and play production procedures to help you function more effectively within the confines, rules, and structure of public school systems.

But before you set foot into a classroom, it's important to understand what school environments are like. I myself will never forget my first day teaching. Totally vulnerable and green, I wondered whether I'd survive the first class. I wasn't frightened of the students—I'd always enjoyed working with adolescents in my hometown's swimming program—it was the *atmosphere*. It was so unsettling I drew a complete blank: I saw the class as a gray blur and read my notes verbatim like a total idiot.

The cold formality of the classroom rattled me. The pleasant, personable attitude and enthusiasm students exhibited outside of class had disappeared. I couldn't relate to this change in behavior. In time I realized the public school environment predisposes all children to this same conventional behavior.

Traditionally, public schools subscribe to a formal code of conduct. From first grade on, children are conditioned to regimentation: students are expected to conduct themselves in an orderly fashion, sit quietly at their desks, and remain emotionally and physically passive in the classroom. This formal conduct also extends into the teacher/student relationship. School protocol requires students to use the titles Mr., Mrs., Miss, or Ms. when addressing a teacher. Teachers in turn are expected to maintain order and discipline and project an image of authority as well as moral integrity through appropriate appearance and behavior. These formal boundaries inevitably force teachers and students into restrictive roles.

Fortunately, teachers today are given considerable latitude in deciding what is appropriate behavior. Few school administrators tell teachers how to dress or how to conduct classes. But there are limits. If a teacher appears too lax with students, allows them to use his first name, or arrives unkempt or improperly dressed, he will risk being reproached.

Teaching is hard work, but teaching within the traditional school framework requires additional stamina on a day-to-day basis to sustain a proper authority image. Fortunately, during free periods the teacher's room becomes a refuge where teachers are allowed to lower defenses, vent their emotions, and be themselves. Students, on the other hand, have few opportunities in this type of setting to unwind and be themselves. They have only short recreation periods in elementary schools, three-minute locker breaks in secondary schools, and the traditional eighteen-minute school lunches.

How well students are conditioned to their formal in-school roles was made clear to me many years ago during a summer vacation. I had enrolled in a ballet class in the town where I taught. The class was a mix of adults and teenagers. While warming up at the ballet bar, I heard two familiar voices, calling, "Hello, Miss P.!" Two of my students had signed up for the same class.

With one leg still on the dance bar, I waved to the girls

and continued to warm up. But I could feel their stares and heard their giggling and whispering as they watched my every move. I found nothing peculiar in what I was doing, so I ignored them. But in subsequent classes, I felt more deeply their sense of discomfort.

It finally occurred to me. They had never seen me out of the school environment and my role as teacher. Until then, all they recognized was an adult authority figure, and this made it awkward for them to be themselves around me.

In contrast, another fourteen-year-old in the same ballet class attended a private school. Not knowing I was a teacher, she had no trouble relating to me. In fact, she was *so* at ease she discussed freely such personal things as the trials and tribulations of a budding summer romance. The day she discovered I was a teacher, a look of perplexed disbelief came over her face and without hesitation she blurted out, "You sure don't *act* like one!"

I took that as a compliment.

Although the reconditioning process was gradual, by summer's end the two girls who'd been my students became less guarded and more at ease. When school resumed in the fall, I again had them in drama. Because they had learned to relate to me as a person, their behavior was noticeably different from that of my other students. They were more cooperative and more responsive in class.

My experience in the ballet class not only shows how deeply ingrained the traditional teacher/student roles are in the minds of adolescents, it also clearly points out the need for teachers and students to relate differently.

Recognizing this need, many systems today are working hard to create a less formal, more nurturing teaching setting by reducing the size of schools as well as the teacher/student ratio. Many *are* succeeding. But until that change occurs nationwide, a drama teacher must learn to function in a regimented learning environment in which the roles of teacher and student are strictly defined, and in which these restrictive student behavior patterns persist.

To teach in this environment, you must break through this structured code of conduct and develop an informal workable relationship with students within *acceptable* boundaries—boundaries in which students *and* school administrations can be comfortable. How? By creating an atmosphere conducive to mutual respect and open personal interaction. This is critical, for the students' individual contributions are what make an activity-oriented subject like drama successful.

If students are to be motivated into action, a drama teacher must break down teacher/student barriers and open up the lines of communication. Knowing how to establish rapport with students is essential, and the first important step towards effective teaching.

12

Developing Rapport with Students

To establish rapport with a class, you have to create an atmosphere conducive to communication and positive inter-action. The best way to open lines of communication is to *just be yourself.*

Avoid defensive posturing. Trying to assert your authority by confronting students with rigid ground rules, for example, will only serve to build a wall between you and your students. Be relaxed and up-front with your class. Your teaching will not be hindered, nor your authority threatened, if students are allowed to see you as a human being with a sense of humor, genuinely interested in them as individuals.

This is especially important at the junior high level where interaction problems commonly occur and where the struggle for independence is the most intense. At this age, adolescents view *any* authority figure as a threat to that independence, thus making thirteen- and fourteen-year-olds the most guarded and critical of their teachers.

First impressions have a lasting effect at this age. Your name, your mannerisms, your physical appearance, the clothes you wear, even the way you talk or walk are especially important to the adolescent in assessing you as a teacher. This may seem cruel and unfair, but don't take it to heart; it's typical of the age, and it's aimed at you "the teacher," and not you "the person."

Regardless of the grade level you teach, to transcend the

teacher facade you must be sensitive to your students' emotional needs and sincere in your desire to communicate. Adolescents are very perceptive, and quickly turned off by pretense. Be honest and open; but don't confuse openness with closeness. Remember, you're a professional: you're not there to be a buddy, you're there to help them grow.

Next, create a relaxed, informal atmosphere. Initially students will be timid and insecure because they don't know what to expect or what is expected of them. Your first goal is to make them comfortable. As already mentioned, Viola Spolin's book, *Improvisation for the Theater*, contains a variety of orientation games and exercises to introduce students to the theater experience and put them at ease.

Keep in mind, however, that traditional orientation exercises focus solely on *students*, while the teacher serves as a non-participating guide or coach. Exercises to help both students *and* teacher become better acquainted should also be used. It is essential that students and teacher adjust *to one another*. In order for adolescents to take performance risks, they must trust and feel comfortable with their teacher; the teacher serves as an emotional safety net. Developing a solid relationship with students is an important and integral part of the orientation process.

One time-tested method I use to make that student connection involves a simple exercise. At the beginning of a new class, I make a mental note of each student's name and face. Once a seating plan is established, I announce to the class I want to test myself by recalling everyone's name without referring to the chart. Adolescents relish seeing teachers put on the spot, but never quite expect one to do so voluntarily. This exercise is not only disarming, but also accomplishes several goals.

By diverting the students' attention to "correcting" the teacher, roles are reversed. Students' apprehensions are defused, and a more relaxed atmosphere is created. Each time I forget or mispronounce a name (which happens *often*), students are allowed to see the fallible and human side of "teacher." More importantly, the exercise forces me to make direct eye contact with each student, breaking down a communication barrier and making future interaction easier.

Observing students' reactions to this exercise also helps me evaluate the attitude and energy level of the class as a whole. I can quickly determine if the class is enthusiastic and dynamic, or shy and inhibited. I can also judge whether a class is slow or quick to react. All these factors play a crucial role in helping gauge the pacing and emotional level needed to motivate students in this particular class. Remember, no two classes are ever alike.

To further break down communication barriers, I have all students perform the following exercise. With the class formed in a circle, each student in turn is required to stand in the center and name all of his classmates. If students know one another, they're required to learn and recall each other's middle name or initial. Again, eye contact is made, and defenses lower.

To further stimulate teacher/student interaction, engage the class in an open forum about theater in general. Lead the discussion by telling students some of your theater experiences and then have each relate their own, including plays they have seen. Open dialogue of this type is the quickest way to size up students, for it helps a teacher evaluate the various personalities that make up the class. By learning theater backgrounds, you're better able to determine the level of drama material that can be introduced. Through this informal interchange, students also lose inhibitions and adjust more readily to an activity-oriented course, enabling you to set the proper tone. Creating a setting in which you and your students can become better acquainted not only helps develop the needed rapport, but also creates an atmosphere where personal interaction and creative expression will flourish.

Once established, how is this rapport maintained? You must evaluate students' overall attitude and energy level on a day-to-day basis. Adolescents are prone to mood swings; therefore no two days in the drama classroom are ever the same. Your students may be exuberant one day, lethargic the next. A drama teacher must be sensitive to these fluxes and capable of redirecting the day's lesson plan. To illustrate, here are simple solutions to two problems you're likely to face:

PROBLEM #1: Your students have spent their last period in a gym class or a school assembly. You have blocking scheduled for class that day. You're ten minutes into the class period, and you're getting nowhere. Students are still keyed up and won't settle down.

SOLUTION: Don't waste time with discipline. Take a few minutes instead and have students perform a few relaxation and concentration exercises in order to calm and refocus them. *Then* continue work on the play.

PROBLEM #2: You have improvisations scheduled for class, but students are unenthused. Tired and listless, they come up with few ideas.

SOLUTION: Get their bodies moving and their minds engaged. Get them on their feet and lead a series of physical warm-ups. If ideas are still slow to come, *assign* specific ideas and have them observe and critique one another's scenes. By tuning in to the general mood, you'll be able to adjust the day's scheduled activity and keep students productive.

13

Rules of Thumb for an Activity-Oriented Class

Creating a relaxed atmosphere in class is important, but never be lax in your approach. An activity-oriented course needs structure; without it little is accomplished, and students lose interest as quickly as you lose control. The degree of structure necessary to maintain control greatly depends on the age and maturity level of students. The younger the adolescent, the more structure and supervision will be required.

Regardless of the age group, the *key* is in knowing how to consistently and quickly focus and engage students in class activities. With only a fifty-minute class period, a drama teacher has little time to waste. Efficient use of time is paramount.

You can keep an activity-oriented class running smoothly day after day by following some basic rules of thumb.

ESTABLISHING CLASSROOM PROCEDURES

First and most important, DEVELOP A DAILY ROUTINE AND STICK TO IT. A curriculum subject such as theater often appears to be recreational in character and often generates relaxed attitudes from students. Talking and socializing quickly replace attentiveness and desire to learn. Both junior and senior high students must understand what is expected of them the moment they enter class. Without a set routine, precious time will be wasted gaining control. Establishing classroom procedures is a must.

Begin by preparing a seating plan. This is especially important when working with large classes, or teaching in junior high. When students report to an assigned seat each day, order is created.

Take attendance as soon as students are seated. Roll call not only indicates class is beginning, but also settles students down before rehearsals or drama activities begin.

When classes are held in a hall or auditorium, confine students to one specific section. Establishing off-limit areas discourages roaming, or exploring backstage and playing with stage equipment. This saves time, and also discourages vandalism.

Teaching drama in the school auditorium or theater may seem like an ideal setting, but interruptions for assemblies and meetings often make this arrangement less than ideal. Adolescents are always unsettled by change, so whenever you're forced to relocate, immediately clear the new area of distracting materials or equipment, and revert to your regular routine.

Establishing procedures will ultimately prevent chaos and quickly promote self-discipline. But more importantly, its purpose is to prepare students for group and self-directed activities.

Next, ESTABLISH A STUDENT CODE OF CONDUCT. Because adolescents are easily embarrassed, they are especially vulnerable in performance situations. Still children in many ways, they are often insensitive and cruel. In order to overcome self-consciousness and nervousness, students must have the respect and support of both their teacher and their fellow classmates. As spectator and performer, they must learn how to exhibit simple acts of courtesy.

No student should be allowed to talk or distract others during activities or scene work. Nor should "harmless" teasing or snide remarks be tolerated. Although behavior of this type is more common in junior high, it does occur on the senior high level as well. In either case, it is disruptive and harmful and should never be permitted.

One good way to maintain order during class activities is to have students critique each other's work when scenes are being presented. A critique sheet with specific areas singled out for comments can be prepared, mimeographed, and distributed to students. (A sample student critique sheet is provided in appendix 3.) If you make critiquing mandatory, and grade students on the critiques they write (or at least give them marks for participation), they are forced to pay attention when others are performing. Critiquing also helps students develop their critical faculties and increases their powers of observation; they learn to recognize and evaluate acting and blocking problems, as well as styles of presentation. Critiquing, therefore, is an invaluable teaching and focusing device.

Once rules of conduct are established, faithfully enforce them. Students should expect reprimands and penalties to be consistent and fairly applied. When a student gets out of line, act quickly. Make no exceptions or your authority will be greatly undermined and more severe discipline will be needed. Be prepared: adolescents will constantly put you to the test.

DEVISE A CONCRETE SYSTEM FOR GRADING.

Junior and senior high students tend to view drama as an activity where grading is incidental. Many school administrations reinforce this view by establishing drama as an non-graded, pass/fail course, assuming there is no objective basis for grading.

This, of course, is untrue.

Although over-emphasizing grades is not the best policy, I

have found that eliminating them altogether sends a message to students that a course has little importance or value in their curriculum.

Remember, adolescents take a course for any of four reasons: 1) they have genuine interest in the subject; 2) they need to fulfill a graduation or college admissions requirement; 3) they are under pressure from family or guidance counselors to take a course; or 4) they simply need to fill their schedule.

Regardless of why a drama course is taken or how enjoyable or interesting it may be, one fact remains: adolescents must be continually coaxed to learn. Learning for learning's sake is rarely enough incentive on the secondary level. Doing well and having a sense of accomplishment, however, always is. Only when standards of quality are clearly established, and students are made to understand how hard work and effort lead to success, can they grow and become self-motivated.

Adolescents need well-defined goals and a clear method to measure progress. The pass/fail system produces the opposite; it adversely affects student responsibilities to a course by diminishing their incentive to do well. The point then is to devise a grading system that qualifies student accomplishment.

I base grades for activity-oriented drama courses on six factors:

1. Quality of work
2. Effort
3. Student interaction
4. Cooperation
5. Attitude
6. Class conduct (when working with junior high students)

As an example, let's say a class is producing a play. Begin by explaining to students their responsibilities to fellow actors and to the play itself. Distribute numbered scripts and explain the importance of caring for them and bringing them to every class.

Adolescents are notoriously forgetful and constantly misplace or lose school materials. Therefore, at the beginning of class, check to see if students have the tools essential for rehearsal. This daily ritual may seem tedious and unnecessary, but you will soon realize how easily rehearsal time can be wasted waiting for students to borrow a pencil or find their script.

Grading should begin at roll call. As each name is called, require students to display their numbered script and a pencil. This guarantees that everyone present has her *assigned* script in hand and not someone else's. Anyone forgetting either script or pencil receives an F for the day.

Theoretically, forgetting play material should bar a student from rehearsal, but one person's irresponsibility should not be allowed to affect a day's rehearsal. Permit the student to participate using an extra script. The F, however, should still stand.

Make sure students understand that at the end of the production, scripts must be returned in good condition. Those badly damaged or lost must be paid for. Adolescents often show more imagination in the *excuses* they make up than in their class work, in their vain attempts to gain sympathy in order to avoid payment. You'll be amazed at some of the lines students come up with. Would *you* believe: "I dropped my script in the garbage disposal," or, "My baby sister threw up on my script at the dinner table while my mother was testing me on lines"? Probably not, but it certainly makes good improvisational material.

The best stories, however, are those that buy students time

to find a script or postpone payment. One of my favorites is: "My script is locked in the trunk of our car and the lock is broken. But don't worry, my father has one on special order, so I should be able to return it in four to six weeks." Hard to argue with that.

The real issue here is accountability, which is difficult to deal with at this age. Many adolescents go out of their way to blame someone else or circumstances "beyond their control," rather than accept personal responsibility. Remain firm, nevertheless. If a student cannot or will not pay for a lost or mutilated script, devise a work duty or assignment to pay the "debt." Of course payment is not the issue; the lesson in responsibility is.

Another good vehicle for grading is scheduling line run-throughs during the course of production. Once blocking is completed, test students weekly on a few pages of dialogue until the entire script is memorized. Grade students on line accuracy and their ability to pick up cues. Deduct a grade point for every cue or line missed.

Regularly scheduled line testing has added benefits. It sharpens concentration and provides a relevant weekly assignment. It also frees students from the script sooner than might otherwise be the case, and gives them more time to focus on characterization and staging during rehearsals.

When you are grading students on their performance in a production, the size of a part should never take precedent over the quality of a student's work. Make this point clear, especially to junior high students, who habitually count and compare the number of lines with other members of their class. If some students feel slighted or show extreme disappointment in a role, assign additional production responsibilities to counter the unavoidable imbalance in part sizes. Grade them on initiative and overall growth.

A student's competence in handling assigned technical

duties—running lights, handling curtain, setting up and striking props and sets, or any other pertinent task—is also a legitimate basis for grading. In junior high, where disruptive behavior is more prevalent, the general attitude and behavior of students during rehearsals or other class activities should be an additional consideration.

Ultimately the question of whether to grade or not to grade remains a philosophical dispute. However, one fact cannot be disputed: Grades *are* effective in motivating students to take a course more seriously. Establishing drama as a graded curriculum subject, therefore, is highly recommended.

And finally, CREATE THE PROPER TEACHING MOMENTUM. Adolescents have an erratic attention span. As a result, a drama teacher must learn to adjust pacing and energy levels to maintain student focus. Remember, it is the teacher and *not* the student who controls this energy level in class activities.

As a rule, the younger the age group, the faster the teaching pace. Regardless of the grade level, check tempo by closely observing behavior. If students are inattentive, restless, or slow to react, pick up the pace; the more energy *you* exert, the more energized the *students* will be. If, on the other hand, students are highly charged, slow down the pace to contain and refocus their energies into productive class activities.

Class procedures and requirements help make learning possible. When you establish standards and rules of behavior, students will become more attentive, more responsible, and better motivated, making individual accomplishment rewarding, and the theater experience worthwhile for all concerned.

MANAGING GROUP ACTIVITIES

Once classroom procedures are established, the next step is managing students when drama activities have begun.

Always have clear-cut curriculum guidelines to follow.

Adolescents need to have well-defined goals and to be shown the necessary steps to attain them. Lesson plans are essential. If the mere mention of a lesson plan makes you break into a cold sweat, here are a few words of advice.

Think of the lesson plan as an organizational tool, a teaching compass, a scratch sheet for formulating teaching ideas and determining educational goals. Personalize the lesson plan to fit your needs. Some teachers use simple outlines written out on index cards; others use more detailed worksheets. Use whatever approach will keep you focused on teaching goals, and will leave you in full control of the day's subject and the direction of the course.

Include in your lesson plan:

1. Name of the course

2. Date and lesson number

3. Objectives, such as:
   a. Educational objective (What practical skill or new insight will students acquire as a result of this lesson?)
   b. General course objective (How does this skill or insight fit into the goals of the course?)
   c. Special course objective (What is the aim of this particular lesson?)

4. Materials for lesson (Textbooks, paper, pencils, art supplies, notebooks, worksheets, etc.)

5. Teaching aids (Movies, slides, blackboard, charts, etc.)

6. Activities (Group warm-ups, scene preparation, group theater games, production projects, etc.)

7. Teaching method (Lecture/discussion, demonstration, group participation, etc.)

8. Lesson outline

9. Homework assignment

10. Evaluation (This can be either a self-evaluation or an evaluation of students. Consider keeping a teaching journal on each class. Comment on student attitude, reaction to the lesson, level of comprehension and participation, etc. Or comment on the success or failure of a lesson or teaching approach, and analyze the areas needing improvement.)

Lesson plans are especially helpful in learning to gauge the appropriate length of lectures or activities, as well as the scope of the material to be covered in a given class period. This is especially important in activity-oriented classes. Learning to estimate how many activities will fill a fifty-minute period takes time. Preparing lesson plans will keep you on track and ensure that specific goals are met.

Always have on hand a list of specific situations for pantomimes and improvisations.

Having little life experience and a limited reference point, adolescents will often be at a loss for ideas. Remember, it takes time to break down inhibitions. For students to be comfortable in group games and acting exercises, they must have enough confidence to initiate their own ideas for skits and scene work. To develop that confidence, they will occasionally need help to spark their imaginations.

Always reinforce verbal instructions with teaching aids.

When working on group projects, provide visual models and illustrations; write directions on the blackboard, or distribute helpful diagrams and instruction sheets. This avoids needless repetition of instructions and provides more class time to answer pertinent questions and supervise group work.

Always know what is happening in your class.

A drama teacher should be able to give students some freedom in group activities without creating confusion in the classroom. For effective control and supervision, you must have what is commonly referred to as "eyes in the back of your head." In other words, develop a form of visual/auditory radar to sense what is happening around you.

There is no magic to this. Simply by expanding your peripheral vision and sharpening your listening skills, you can decipher and keep track of many activities at one time. Let's say a group of students are performing while the rest of the class is sitting and observing. A good teacher can concentrate on the scene, and at the same time know if the rest of the class is paying attention. Of course the most obvious way is to physically position yourself at the back of the class, where you have all students in full view. But this isn't always possible or even desirable, especially when students are broken into small groups or engaged in activities in different areas of the classroom.

The best way to supervise many activities at once is to *listen* and *observe*. For example, when students are allotted time to prepare for scenes or exercises, focus in on the overall tone and volume of group discussions; a lot of laughter, loud discourse, or guarded whispering may indicate socializing rather than productive work. Attitude and body language also send very clear messages. Students slouching in their seats, leaning on their elbows, or mindlessly doodling on paper or a notebook may not be paying attention; sighing, or unfocused eyes gazing into space may be signs of disengagement or boredom. Learning to *read* students from a distance makes it possible to differentiate between productive and counterproductive group discussions and activities. When observing practice teachers, I can tell whether the energy level or pacing of the class is appropriate by simply focusing in on sounds in the class. With practice and experience, anyone can develop these invaluable skills and use them effectively.

Managing difficulties also arise when producing class plays. For example, what do you do with students who are required to sit for long periods of time waiting to be blocked? This is an issue every drama teacher faces, for the problem of boredom is real and needs to be dealt with effectively.

There is a solution. Assign in-class drama worksheets and projects during these tedious periods; put together a series of theater crossword puzzles on subject matter already covered; or have students write out a character sketch. You can use this time for creative writing by having students write out ideas for skits, or create original dialogue for a scene or one-act play. Or involve students in production work that can be completed during class time, such as building simple props, designing a simple set piece, or drawing production posters. Any task or assignment accomplished quietly during a rehearsal will be effective.

The goal is to engage students in a theater-related activity during tedious blocking and technical rehearsals when it's impossible to focus their attention on the play. This is especially important at the junior high level where the attention span is shorter and where disruptive behavior is most common. But with a little effort and the right preparation and organization, an activity-oriented class can be kept running smoothly.

Managing class activities effectively is essential in gaining optimal productivity from students. Good class management teaches adolescents how to work both independently and cooperatively during an allotted period of time, and allows you to achieve your educational goals as well as to complete the practical steps involved in a theatrical production.

Part V

THE PLAY PRODUCTION PROCESS

. . . It is a question of making the theater, in the proper sense of the word, a function; something as localized and precise as the circulation of the blood in the arteries . . . and this is to be accomplished by a thorough involvement. . . .

—Antonin Artaud,
The Theater and Its Double

ADJUSTING TO EDUCATIONAL THEATER

To mount a show in professional theater, trained artists and skilled craftsmen are always available to get the job done. But a high school drama teacher is in charge of *every* aspect and phase of production. The long list of responsibilities can be overwhelming; it was overwhelming for me when I started teaching.

I had difficulty adjusting to the teaching mode of educational theater. Frustrated by my students' inexperience, I became impatient when they failed to accomplish tasks as fast or as well as I thought they should. In my zeal to produce the best show possible, I made the mistake of handling most of the production work and depending on the help of qualified professionals.

For a time this approach was successful. But I soon realized that doing the work of ten or more people would quickly lead to burnout. More importantly, by not giving students every available opportunity to experience and learn from production work, I was failing them. Therefore, I was failing as a teacher.

In time I learned how to make the production process work for me as well as for my students. This is what I learned: Successful productions at the secondary level involve organization and know-how in delegating work and authority. But the most critical factor is knowing how to save time and money by making use of school and community resources.

In the following chapters, we will examine in detail each phase of production and ways to make the production process easier. In order to understand this process fully, I've divided this discussion into three parts. Chapter 14 shows how to organize and handle a student company within the school framework. Chapter 15 points out common production prob-lems and money-saving solutions. Finally, chapter 16 dis-cusses the special requirements of the high school musical.

Let's get started.

14

Creating a Production Company

Every drama teacher must work within the structure of a school system. By following school regulations and scheduling procedures you can avoid needless frustrations and delays. The following steps are designed to help minimize problems and keep the production process on track.

▶ **Step 1: ATTEND TO SCHOOL BUSINESS FIRST.**

Before setting up a production schedule, you must clear all performance dates with the principal's and/or superintendent's office. You don't want to conflict with other school or community activities that have scheduled use of the auditorium or other facilities you plan to use. Next, talk to the custodians about their work schedules and lock-up procedures. Remember, they're in charge of security as well as building maintenance. You'll need their cooperation to gain access to buildings and facilities during after-school hours.

Once these small but important details are taken care of, the production process can begin.

▶ **Step 2: ORGANIZE A PRODUCTION STAFF.**

As producer, you are responsible for appropriating funds, preparing the budget, and paying the royalties and bills. As director, your main task is to train and inspire adolescents to recognize and develop their full potential as actors or production technicians. Your artistic goal is to faithfully adhere to the playwright's intentions in regards to the play's theme and character relationships. It is also your responsibility to instill enthusiasm and an *esprit de corps* among company members. Building morale is essential for cohesion; and part of that process involves coordinating all of the play elements into a unified whole. As head of the production staff, your directorial duties are as follows:

- Select a play and set performance dates.
- Prepare a calender of required production work and deadlines.
- Determine the mood and overall production style (costumes, settings, props, furniture, and lighting), and style of presentation.
- Prepare a promptbook which includes:
    General blocking.
    Actors' entrance cues.
    Set changes.
    Sound and lighting cues.
- Prepare an audition sheet as well as a printed form containing the play synopsis and character descriptions for prospective auditioners.
- Cast the play.
- Plot a rehearsal overview (commonly called a *god chart*) that projects the first week's schedule through the post-production strike.
- Prepare weekly rehearsal schedules.
- Coordinate and run all technical and dress rehearsals.
- Keep order and calm nerves backstage before the opening night curtain.
- Hand the reins of responsibility over to the stage manager as places are called.
- Join the audience and enjoy the show.

If the job of overseeing all of the production elements is too overwhelming, buy a director's notebook to help you get organized. One that I especially like is sold through the Eldridge Publishing play catalogue (for the address, see appendix 8). This three-ring binder contains over fifty pages of checklists, schedules, and practical tips to guide you through the entire production process from auditions to opening night. It contains such items as a sample production schedule, planning calendars, audition notices, tryout sheets, evaluation forms, expense logs, templates for set designs, prop planning sheets, publicity planning, program checklists, inventory sheets, and much more.

Although you are in charge of all phases of production, your ultimate goal should be to organize and prepare students to handle most of the work, keeping yourself in a supervisory position. To do this effectively, lay the groundwork for developing an efficient, self-perpetuating work system whereby older, more experienced students help teach and supervise those younger and less experienced in production work.

As discussed in an earlier chapter, an apprenticeship training system is an excellent learning experience for all concerned. Students are given the opportunity to become role models as they develop the skills and maturity needed to handle the responsibilities that surround every production.

Setting up a production staff within this type of teaching framework initially takes time and patience, but I guarantee it will make play production easier and more rewarding in the long run. As students learn to accept added responsibilities, they become capable of handling and solving minor production problems and are less dependent on you. Delegating authority in this way allows you to control and oversee the entire production more effectively.

A well-organized staff also has built-in benefits. It provides students with a concrete framework for a more cooperative effort. They learn to work towards a common goal and to work through personal conflicts as they occur. And whenever personality clashes or disagreements arise, students learn not to dwell on why or how a problem was created or who was the cause, but instead focus on solving the problem for the good of the production. Through the staff framework students also come to understand that each person is an integral part of the whole, and if one member falters in his or her responsibilities, *everyone* is affected.

When you set out to organize a production staff, begin by making a list of staff members needed. Use the list below as a guide, and adjust or modify job requirements to meet the maturity level, talent, and skills of your students.

The following is a list of specific staff duties and responsibilities readily handled by high school students. Included are basic requirements to consider when evaluating students' abilities and their sense of responsibility. Also listed are suggestions for finding and selecting the most qualified people in your school.

STAGE MANAGER

STUDENT REQUIREMENTS: Choose a student who is mature enough to assert authority and who is conscientious, flexible, adept at handling details, and receptive to taking and giving orders. Since the stage manager must be able to handle production problems as they arise during the run of a show, find someone who works well under pressure. Because of the responsibilities involved, the stage manager should be free of all other after-school commitments, such as regularly scheduled sport practices or a part-time job.

Remember, your stage manager is your "right hand man"—make sure you choose someone you can depend on and with whom you can feel comfortable working.

PRE-PRODUCTION DUTIES:

- Distributes audition information and scripts for readings.
- Posts weekly rehearsal schedule.
- Takes attendance at rehearsal.
- Notifies actors absent from rehearsal.
- Sets up scenes for rehearsal.
- Provides actors with essential props during rehearsal.
- Prompts lines (unless there is a separate prompter).
- Prepares a stage manager's promptbook which includes:
    General blocking.
    Actors' entrance cues.
    Set changes.
    Sound and curtain cues.

PRODUCTION DUTIES:

- Takes complete charge backstage during performances.
- Calls time before curtain.
- Checks to see that all scenery, props, and lighting are in order.
- Calls the actors to their places.
- Follows book.
- Gives entrance warnings to actors, as well as curtain and sound warnings and go cues to backstage crews.

TECHNICAL DIRECTOR

STUDENT REQUIREMENTS: Find a student with basic carpentry skills who is capable of handling minor problems as they arise, who gets along well with others, and who can organize and delegate projects. Because of the responsibilities involved, your technical director should be present for all

Behind-the-scenes glimpses: A stage manager shows the strain of a long, tedious rehearsal, while the director leads actors and the crew through their cues in a technical rehearsal.

The lighting board provides technically gifted students with an important role in any play.

scheduled construction work and should therefore be free of all other after-school commitments.

DUTIES:

- Takes inventory of available lighting equipment, building supplies, and materials with appropriate crew heads.
- Orders building supplies and materials.
- Oversees and assists construction work.
- Makes certain all set designs are executed accurately.
- Reports major construction problems to the supervising adult or teacher.

SOURCES TO CONSIDER: If a qualified student is not available, try the school industrial arts department. The shop teacher may be willing to help build sets, or may recommend someone who can. Ask for a list of his best students. If all else fails, students may have parents or relatives with basic carpentry skills who are willing to donate time to help teach and supervise construction work. You have nothing to lose by asking.

CREW HEADS:

The set head, costume head, prop master, lighting head, and publicity head share the following responsibilities.

DUTIES:

• Recruit and organize student crew members.

• Organize, delegate, and supervise crew work.

• Attend all scheduled production staff meetings.

• Attempt to solve production problems before contacting the supervising adult or teacher for ultimate solutions.

Set Head

STUDENT REQUIREMENTS: To meet production deadlines you will need a responsible student with basic carpentry skills and good organizational skills. One who can use time efficiently, teach crew members necessary skills, and assign projects they can handle and hopefully enjoy. Remember, when students are enthusiastic about a building assignment, they are more likely to produce quality work. Again, because of the responsibilities involved, your set head must be free of all after-school commitments.

PRE-PRODUCTION DUTIES:

• Works closely with the technical director.

• Builds or acquires necessary sets.

• Assigns and rotates building responsibilities among construction crew members.

- Is responsible for the care, maintenance, and storage of all hand and power tools after daily crew work.
- Maintains order and cleanliness throughout the building process.
- Makes sure an adult is present when potentially dangerous power tools (and power saws of any kind) are used.
- Attends run-throughs to determine set locations and scene changes.

PRODUCTION DUTIES:

- Organizes and coordinates stage hands to set up and strike scenery.
- Supervises set changes during the run of the show.

Costume Head

STUDENT REQUIREMENTS: Whether or not you make some or all costumes, find someone who sews well or who is at least competent to adapt or alter an everyday article of clothing into an appropriate period or character costume. It is also helpful if the student owns or has access to a sewing machine outside of school, in the event there's a problem scheduling use of the school's sewing room.

PRE-PRODUCTION DUTIES:

- Determines the number of costumes needed.
- Makes up a costume chart indicating the characters of the play, the scenes in which they appear, and a description of costumes needed in each scene.
- Compiles a list of measurements and sizes of each cast member.
- Sews or acquires needed costumes.
- Organizes crew members to serve as dressers during the run of the show when needed.

SOURCES TO CONSIDER: If you have trouble finding a costume head, approach your school's home economics department. The sewing teachers will be your best source. Cast and crew members may also have friends or relatives with sewing skills who are willing to help.

Prop Master or Mistress

STUDENT REQUIREMENTS: Again, pick a student with good organizational skills and competence in handling details. If possible, find someone with a driver's license and access to a car; the prop crew may then work independently, picking up borrowed furniture and needed props after school.

DUTIES:

- Makes or acquires necessary prop items and furniture.
- Compiles a general prop list detailing each item required, who acquired it, and from whom it is borrowed.
- Attends rehearsals to determine location of furniture, and placement of hand and stage props in each scene.
- Makes up a prop chart stating what furniture and props are needed in each scene and where they are to be placed.
- Organizes and coordinates crew members for setting up and striking furniture and props during the run of the show.
- Makes certain all borrowed items are accounted for and safely returned at the end of the show by the same crew members who acquired them.

Publicity Head(s)

Publicity duties in my productions cover four distinct areas: promotion, posters, tickets/play program, and box office. Since different talents and skills are required for each area, the following duties are best fulfilled by assigning each to a different student.

STUDENT REQUIREMENTS: The top priority is to find someone personable and aggressive enough to promote the show and get an ad campaign off the ground. You also need an artistic student to design a production poster. To organize and lay out the tickets and play program, select someone with good typing skills, preferably proficient in the use of a computer or a word processor. The student in charge of box office must be reliable, trustworthy, and competent in math in order to keep accurate sales records.

PROMOTION DUTIES:

- Arranges radio spots, newspaper promotions, or other publicity schemes to publicize the play.
- Organizes crew members to solicit ads for the play's program.

POSTER DUTIES:

- Designs a poster for advertising the play.
- Organizes the distribution and hanging of posters around the school and community.

TICKET/PROGRAM DUTIES:

- Lays out tickets and play program for printing.

BOX OFFICE DUTIES:

- Is in charge of advanced ticket sales and box office sales.
- Recruits ushers to hand out programs and sell refreshments during intermissions.

SOURCES TO CONSIDER: If you can't find someone to design your poster, ask the art teachers for leads. The typing and bookkeeping teachers are your best source for students qualified to handle box office. You can ask the journalism or computer teachers for the names of students experienced in layout work or desktop publishing to handle your program. If your school has a media center, that is an ideal resource.

Lighting Head

STUDENT REQUIREMENTS: You will need a technically inclined student capable of handling and hanging lighting equipment and running a lighting board. The lighting head must also be able to coordinate and train a lighting crew as well as supervise crew members during the run of the show. Note that because of school liability problems, many school systems forbid students to climb extension ladders and catwalks. In this case, arrange to have custodians hang and focus lights. Your lighting crew should assist in order to gain as much hands-on experience as the school will allow.

DUTIES:

- Responsible for hanging, gelling, and focusing lights.
- Attends run-throughs prior to production week to study the script and determine the basic lighting requirements and special effects needed.
- Prepares a script with lighting warnings and go cues.
- Gives lighting cues during the run of the show.

SOURCES TO CONSIDER: Ask the industrial arts teachers for a list of students training to be electrician's helpers or apprentices. Also ask the audio-visual department director for the names of those who help distribute and maintain school equipment. If there's a TV/broadcasting studio or a video department in your school, chances are there will be students trained to operate television, video, and lighting equipment, giving you an excellent source of technically trained students to choose from.

Although the staff requirements listed above are straight-forward, nothing is etched in stone. Learn to accommodate students' needs and schedules when necessary. *Be flexible.*

Also keep in mind that many qualified students, because of shyness or lack of self-confidence, will often be reluctant to step forward. When students are recommended by teachers, make a point of approaching them yourself. With a little encouragement, you'll be surprised how many become involved when asked directly.

Staff positions involve a great deal of input and responsibility. Any recruits not enrolled in a drama class or directly involved in theater should be compensated in some way for their work. Either negotiate extra credit with their teacher, or at the very least, offer them complementary tickets and acknowledge their contribution in the play program.

Once your staff list is completed, make it available to students before every production. Have both staff openings and audition dates included in the school's morning announcements and daily bulletin at least *two weeks* before scheduled auditions. This will give students ample time to decide whether they want to work on the production, audition for a part, or do both.

▶ Step 3: GET THE MOST OUT OF THE AUDITION PROCESS.

Whenever possible, allow students to sign out scripts a week or two before auditions. On the day of tryouts, include with the audition sheet a synopsis of the play and a character sketch stating the age ranges and types of each character. Indicate whether a role is major or minor, or a speaking or non-speaking part. The more information you provide students about the play, the more effective the audition process will be.

When putting together an audition sheet, keep in mind

that the more information you gather about each auditioning student, the easier the casting will be. The sample audition sheet on the following page provides essential information for casting a secondary level production.

Question five on the sheet is critical because adolescents are often unaware of the time needed for rehearsals and crew work. They can easily over-extend themselves without realizing it. With this information, you will avoid casting students in major roles who are unable to attend regular rehearsals, and cast instead those with more flexible after-school commitments.

Asking students whether they will accept *any* part (question two) eliminates the need to recast roles. Remember, you're dealing with fragile egos. If you have a clear understanding—*before* casting a show—of how students feel about parts and about the overall role they wish to play in your production, you can often prevent unnecessary conflicts and aggravations later on. However, students do change their minds; so once the cast list is posted, require that they initial the role if the part is accepted.

By asking students if they are willing to work on a production crew (question six), the audition sheet serves a dual purpose. Not only does it provide necessary information for casting a show and for setting up attendance files once auditions are over, it's also a valuable source of information for organizing production crews. Once the show is cast, you can cut off the audition notes section, and keep the remaining data on file for the stage manager and crew heads.

In the audition notes section, write down all of the information you need to evaluate each student's performance. When judging a student's suitability for a role, consider:

• Physical appearance and body type (Does he look the part?) *Audition notation:* too tall _____ too short _____ too young _____ too old _____ other _____

Sample Audition Sheet

AUDITION INFORMATION

Name:

Address:

Telephone :

Grade: Age: Height: Weight:

1. Which role(s) are you auditioning for?

2. Would you accept any part?

3. Have you ever been in a play before? If so, list plays and parts.

4. Do you have any special skills (such as dancing, acrobatics, playing a musical instrument, sewing, singing, drawing, etc.)?

5. Please list all after-school activities you have Monday through Friday from 3:00 P.M. to 6:00 P.M.

6. Which of the following crews would you be willing to work on (please circle three, and number according to preference):

   sets   props   costumes   lighting   publicity

7. Circle study period(s):
   Period: 1   2   3   4   5   6   7   8   9

8. List names of subject teachers:
   1.   4.   7.
   2.   5.   8.
   3.   6.   9.

(Do not write below this line)

- -

Audition Notes:

- Voice and diction (Does he have a good stage voice?)
  Audition notation: too weak _____ too tight _____
  monotone _____ expressive _____ other _____

- Role interpretation (Does he project the character's personality?)
  Audition notation: energetic _____ emotionally
  intense _____ imaginative _____ arouses interest _____
  other _____

- Posture and movement (Does he have good stage presence?)
  Audition notation: agile _____ loose _____ fluid _____
  stiff _____other _____

- Role possibilities

   Make note of each auditioner's strengths and weaknesses to determine the areas that need work and improvement. When there is a large number of students auditioning, jot down a word or two about the looks of students you don't know, or describe something they're wearing; it will help you remember who they are when working out the cast list. Also be sure the students you select to play opposite one another are not only compatible physically, but also compatible in terms of their maturity and emotional depth. For example, a male freshman who *looks* older may not have the emotional maturity to successfully play opposite a female senior. It should be feasible for students to create believable roles *and* relationships in a play.
   When casting a high school production, consider the talent and growth potential of students trying out, but also take into account their attitudes and feelings about participating and becoming involved. A talented student who shows little interest in attending regular rehearsals and crew meet-

ings will be less valuable than one who is less talented, but eager to participate.

Because these additional factors need consideration, schedule as much audition time as you need. No matter what days of the week auditions are held, I always schedule final callbacks after school on Friday. This allows me to keep students as long as I need them without cutting into homework time, so important on a school night. It also gives the added benefit of a weekend to cast the show.

One final reminder: Keep auditions open. Open auditions are good publicity for a show. They give students the opportunity to see others perform on stage and offer moral support to those auditioning.

▶ **Step 4: MAXIMIZE REHEARSAL TIME.**

The key to any successful production is making sure students consistently show up for rehearsal. To keep absenteeism down, have in place a consistent and well-organized system for notifying actors of rehearsal times, taking attendance, and checking on absentees.

Begin by designating a specific place where weekly rehearsal schedules can be posted and picked up weekly. Make them available by Thursday or Friday for the following week; this will give cast members ample time to change or rearrange job hours or other after-school activities.

Second, have the stage manager check the absence list daily and maintain an updated file of each cast member's class schedule, home address, phone number, and after-school commitments.

Third, establish clear-cut rules regarding rehearsal attendance. Because your production is first and foremost a *school* activity, any rules devised must take into account your school's attendance and eligibility policies. Although rules will vary, the following generally apply:

RULE 1: If a cast member is absent from school, she cannot attend that day's rehearsal.

RULE 2: If a cast member receives a failing grade at the end of a term, she becomes ineligible and cannot be in the production.

To keep abreast of your cast's academic standings, distribute copies of the cast list to all faculty members at mid-semester and request notification of any student listed who is in danger of failing a course. This enables you to warn cast members and do whatever is necessary to remedy the situation. Often the threat of losing a part after weeks of rehearsals is by itself enough motivation to improve grades. But if not, cover yourself by having understudies available. You don't want surprises when the ineligible list comes along. By then, it's too late.

▶ **Step 5: ESTABLISH A CUT POLICY AND STICK TO IT.**

Any cut policy established should be strict but fair. It should keep students accountable, yet be flexible enough to accommodate unavoidable circumstances or unexpected events.

The cut system I've adopted breaks down absences into justified and unjustified cuts. A student is allowed seven justified and three unjustified cuts before he is out of a show.

An absence is recorded as a *justified* cut when a cast member

a. is listed on the day's absence list, or

b. informs either the stage manager or the drama teacher in *advance* about an appointment (doctor, orthodontist, etc.) or an unexpected event (called home, required to report to detention or to a teacher, etc.).

Five justified cuts due to *school absences* warrant a conference. I issue a warning, then determine whether the student's absence from school is due to illness or other personal problems. By talking with the student, I can determine whether the problem can be resolved or if the cast member must be replaced.

An absence is recorded as an unjustified cut when a cast member

a. is *not* listed on the day's absence list;
b. fails to notify the stage manager or drama teacher of his intended absence from rehearsal;
c. cannot be reached at home by phone (this for students who sometimes forget or confuse rehearsal dates); or
d. has received three marks for tardiness. (When a student is more than fifteen minutes late for rehearsal, he is marked tardy, unless he first notifies me or the stage manager about the delay.)

When a cast member has two unjustified cuts, or one due to tardiness, I meet with the individual to issue a warning and discover his reasons for absence or lateness. Again, there may be a problem in school or at home, or the student may simply be losing interest.

This follow-up process is vital no matter what cut policy you implement, for it keeps students accountable and acutely aware of the responsibility and commitment involved, and it also keeps you informed of the status and whereabouts of cast members when they don't show up for rehearsal.

Of course, the best way to minimize absenteeism is to keep students interested and motivated. When actors are not needed on stage, give them something to do. Have them run lines, or assign crew work until their scenes come up.

Remember, keeping students productive helps keep the process moving forward.

▶ **Step 6: PREPARE IN ADVANCE FOR PRODUCTION WEEK.**

As anyone in theater knows, production week is the most demanding and intense period of the rehearsal process. Because of the concentrated time and coordinated effort required, full cooperation of the cast and crew is essential. To make this process easier and less taxing, you also need the cooperation of the faculty, the school administration, and the maintenance department. So before production week begins, take care of school matters.

Clear all afternoon and evening rehearsals with the front office to avoid last-minute conflicts in the use of school facilities. Notify school custodians of the nature and length of evening rehearsals in order to ensure access to buildings and classrooms and to avoid being locked in or out of school. Also notify parents of all evening rehearsals and performances so that transportation to and from school can be arranged.

Most high schools require the presence of a policeman at large functions. Unless your school has its own security service, arrange to have a police officer on duty opening night and at subsequent performances. Call your local police station a week or two in advance to put in a request and have them bill your school. Police officers assigned special duty are usually paid an hourly wage which varies from community to community. If your school does not have a special fund to pay for these services, include enough money in your budget to cover the cost.

To avoid the needless frustration of rehearsal absenteeism, impress upon cast and crews the importance of clearing their schedules of all after-school activities and appointments. Give older students with after-school jobs enough notice to adjust or switch work hours.

More important, advise them to take full advantage of school study periods and weekends to complete homework. Any scheduled tests, papers, or projects due during production week should be prepared and studied for in advance. If necessary, however, don't be afraid to approach faculty members. They will often show flexibility and understanding in rescheduling tests for key cast and crew members if and when the need arises.

No doubt scheduling compromises will need to be made. The point is to keep them at a minimum.

▶ **Step 7: ADJUST TECHNICAL AND DRESS REHEARSALS TO MEET STUDENT NEEDS.**

During technical rehearsals, a good deal of time is spent working out production problems while the cast sits around waiting for cues. This can be lethal on the secondary school level. With the full cast present it is difficult to solve technical problems without confusion and disruption. Here are some suggestions to make these rehearsals less taxing:

• Run your cue-to-cue rehearsal with a minimum of actors present. You'll be able to focus your attention on coordinating technical crews without having to supervise and deal with bored, disgruntled actors. Once cues have been worked out, schedule a tech run-through with the full cast present.

• Schedule evening rehearsals as early as possible. You don't want to keep students up too late on school nights and provoke the wrath of parents, especially those of younger cast members.

• Make sure students are secure in their parts and duties. Spell out cast requirements for makeup and costume maintenance, as well as preparation procedures for backstage crews.

- When possible, schedule an extra tech/dress rehearsal without makeup. This gives students more time to adjust to props, scenery, and costume changes, and buys more time to solve last-minute technical problems.
- And finally, give your cast as much performing experience as possible. Treat your dress rehearsal like a performance and invite a group of people to attend.

▶ **Step 8: KEEP PRE-PERFORMANCE ACTIVITIES RUNNING SMOOTHLY OPENING NIGHT.**

Once opening night arrives, your main task will be to soothe and calm nervous stomachs and pre-performance jitters. Give students all the support and encouragement they

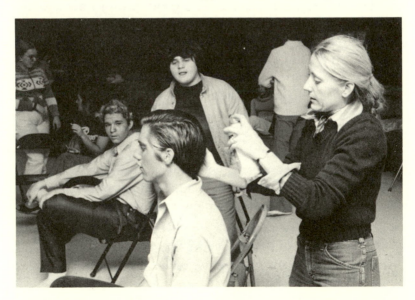

Although make-up should be handled by the backstage crew recruited for that purpose, a director may have to step in and pinch-hit.

need. The energy level of adolescent actors runs high and stems from the sheer excitement of performing. Learn to contain and focus this energy for performance.

Eliminate needless distractions. Have actors report directly to assigned dressing rooms upon arrival; don't allow them to roam the lobby or the house. Forbid visitors backstage. Once the house opens, keep actors out of the stage area until places are called. Otherwise, they'll be peering out of the curtain to see if friends and relatives have arrived.

Have everything in place in the lobby ahead of time. Programs should be ready for distribution and refreshment tables set up for intermission. Ushers should be instructed in advance as to their appearance, conduct, and appropriate duties before and during performances. To add a touch of professionalism and class, I require boys to wear jackets, ties, and slacks (no jeans), and girls to wear dresses or skirts. This not only gives students a greater sense of personal pride and responsibility, it also teaches important lessons in social conduct and etiquette—experiences greatly needed at this age.

Above all, handle any last minute production problems calmly and efficiently. Remember, your attitude in dealing with a crisis will directly affect the performance of your cast and crews. Avoid making any major changes once the show has gelled. This only shakes the confidence of a company of this age and creates undue stress.

Finally, before you hand the show over to your stage manager on opening night, make a point of gathering the entire company in an offstage area (perhaps the music room) for a pep talk. This is a great morale booster and refocuses young actors who are by now riding high on adrenaline. After thanking various key members for their hard work, perhaps small gifts of apppreciation might be exchanged; offer a few last words of advice and encouragement, and then circle together for a rallying cheer. Be sure to remind your company to *enjoy* themselves. Isn't that what theater's all about? Hopefully, as you watch the opening night performance, remembering the weeks of hard work spent nurturing and developing young talent and seeing how much your students have grown, you will come to understand, as I have, how rewarding play production at the secondary level can be.

15

Handling Production Elements: Money-Saving Options

Although production work requires considerable time and manpower, the real key to success is knowing how to make the most of the funds at your disposal. While students hone their skills in theater craft, work to build a basic stock of costumes, props, and scenery for use in future productions. But don't stop there; take advantage of any and all available school and community resources.

If there's not an established drama department or club in your school, ask the principal how plays were produced in the past. There may be old flats, backdrops, or even costumes tucked away somewhere that could be salvaged and used. Talk to the custodians. They'd know all of the nooks and crannies where scenery might be stored. Once you have a clear picture of what there is to work with, meet with your technical director and production crew heads and compile lists of additional items and materials needed.

Next, develop a resource network.

Whether you need props, fabric, costumes, or building materials, schedule a company production meeting and go over lists with your cast and crews. Students can often supply items or materials from home, or know of a friend or relative who might be of help. Parents especially can be overwhelmingly generous and supportive. So don't purchase anything until you see what kind of response you get. You may be pleasantly surprised. I know I always am.

For example, in one production the father of the technical

director owned a lumber company and contributed all the wood and building materials for our set. In another instance, an actor's father who owned a garment business donated fabrics and gave a substantial discount on chiffons and taffetas for a production of *My Fair Lady*. The parents of another actor in the same production managed a formalwear store and provided morning suits and dress tails at minimal charge in exchange for a full-page ad in the program.

At the very least, there will always be parents willing to loan or donate tools, used clothing and accessories, old furniture, and other needed materials. There may even be a supportive parent or relative willing to help make costumes or help in construction work.

Expand your network into the community.

Contact local theater groups and college drama departments. You may be able to rent or borrow lighting equipment at a nominal fee, or a special prop, costume, or set piece when the need arises. Try different stores and supply houses for the best prices. Get a list of local suppliers from home economics and industrial arts teachers.

The more money you save, the better.

If a play requires many period or character costumes, scout local thrift shops and rummage sales for basic skirts, dresses, and pants to build on. Find a notions store where ribbons, laces, trims, and fabrics are sold in large quantities at discount prices. You'd be amazed how easy it is to transform an everyday item of clothing into an appropriate costume using a few basic notions and art supplies.

For example, in my production of *My Fair Lady* the gowns designed for the Ascot scene were built by adding trims, laces, and fabric to the bodices, sleeves, and hems of simple dresses. The elegant picture hats were created by cutting large donut shapes out of poster board and placing them over the smaller rims of inexpensive beach hats. They were edged and decorated with fabric, ribbon, and lace using staples and glue. The parasols were made by gathering taffeta edged with lace and wrapping and attaching it to painted wooden dowels. And—voila!

If set and costume designs are needed, students from the art department, especially those interested in broadening their portfolios for college, will usually be willing to draft and execute drawings. Over the years, I've had many talented students volunteer to draft and execute scrim and set designs. They received extra credit in art, and I benefited by having a small stock of scenery and original backdrops used in more musicals than would seem possible.

How simple or elaborate your production will be depends of course on the skill and talent available. But don't be afraid

These elaborate costumes and accessories in "My Fair Lady" were made inexpensively, using thrift-shop dresses, basic notions, and supplies from the school art department.

of a challenge. Your only limits will be those you impose on yourself and your students. With a little help, a few basic materials, and a lot of ingenuity, a play's production requirements need not be overwhelming or expensive.

Stage lighting can be as elaborate as that found in professional theater with its array of spots, floods, and specials, or as simple as overhead lights operated from an on-and-off switch. The lighting found in most school auditoriums falls somewhere in between.

Many school auditoriums are equipped with basic strip lights and a simple dimmer board. Extremely practical and versatile in school settings, this type of equipment provides ample lighting for programs and assemblies, but an inadequate flat wash when used for plays. Reds, blues, and ambers used separately or in combination are effective for setting moods and creating special effects.

If stage lighting is less than adequate, your options are to buy (possibly through your school's building maintenance budget, so look into it!), rent, or borrow what you need. Or once again make use of good old ingenuity. When desperate enough, I've put together makeshift lighting using 150 par 38 lamps and six-inch coffee cans, and have on occasion used Christmas and flash lights to create different effects.

For ideas and suggestions in this area, an excellent book to use is James Hull Miller's *Stage Lighting in the Boondocks*, 3d edition, a layman's handbook of simple methods for lighting productions with limited resources. The Holtje and Mayr book, *Putting on the School Play: A Complete Handbook*, also lists ways to get maximum results with minimum lighting and cost. If you are more ambitious and have a basic knowledge of electricity, or the cooperation of the industrial arts teachers, consider building some of your own equipment. Theodore Fuchs's book, *Home-Built Lighting Equipment: For the Small Stage*, provides a material list and scaled drawings for constructing spotlights, olivettes, striplights, footlights, and borderlights, as well as scene projectors and a basic dimmer board. The point is to consider what is feasible, available, and affordable in your teaching situation.

The bottom line in lighting is visibility—you have to make sure actors can be clearly seen. When stage lighting is minimal and your only choice is to use what's available, put actors in closer contact with the audience and allow for more interaction. Select a play that is geared to (or easily adapted to) a more theatrical style—one emphasizing stage action rather than mood or visual effect.

For a realistic play, create more intimacy by using a thrust stage, or by moving your production to a different locale (say, the gym or cafeteria) and staging your production in the round. Use whatever approach will allow actors to connect with the audience. One small consolation: When stage lighting is not used, money *will* be saved on makeup; the less intense the lighting, the less makeup your actors will need.

In terms of publicity, a promotional campaign can be approached in a variety of ways. The most common tool is the production poster. You can make it a professionally illustrated design or a simple mimeographed flyer. It all depends on what you can afford. One simple way to get a professional-looking poster at minimal cost is to organize a poster contest through the art department. You'll have a variety of well-designed posters to choose from and you'll be providing the artistic student an opportunity to exhibit her talent throughout the school and community.

The industrial arts teacher or art teacher can often recommend a printing company with reasonable rates. Or perhaps they will print your posters, tickets, and programs for free or at a reduced cost in the school printing shop. You'll not only save money, you'll also promote good will and cooperation among school departments.

Winthrop Jr. + Sr. High Schools

present—

BYE, BYE BIRDIE!

May 9, 10
8:00 P.M.
Memorial Auditorium

Holding a contest for poster design of a show is a potential draw for students not otherwise interested in drama. It also helps to form an alliance of the drama and art departments—useful for many aspects of a production.

During production week, include the dates of your show in the community event announcements of local radio and television stations. Most stations provide this service at no charge. Since local newspapers are always interested in school and community events, submit a few articles about the production to the press. Include a synopsis of the play; the names of lead players; a short profile on the director, choreographer, musical director, etc.; the dates, place, and times of performances; and the price of tickets or a phone number to call for ticket information.

Also check out community activities. Fairs, bake sales, and bazaars provide free publicity opportunities. For example, at one local bazaar, students showed up in costume and sold tickets for their spring musical, while another student paraded in a clown costume selling helium balloons printed with the name and dates of the show.

Remember, cast and crew members also want the production to succeed. They are more than willing to devote time and energy to publicizing their show, and when given a chance, they will come up with ingenious ideas. So always allow student input when planning publicity strategies.

Because a production is first and foremost a school activity, heavily promote your play within the school system. Have production dates announced in classes and printed on daily bulletins during production week. If you're producing a children's play or a musical, contact the elementary school principals and include the dates in their announcements as well. Provide teachers with play posters or mailers for students to take home, or make arrangements to have a short preview of the play presented at each school. And whenever possible, schedule a special Saturday matinee.

The more students you can draw to performances, the better your drama program will appear in the eyes of the administration, school board, and community. Remember,

A promotional campaign needs to be planned for show publicity. Students often come up with ingenious ideas, like this one, to bring the message into the greater community.

your goal is not only to draw a paying audience to cover royalties and expenses, but also to win support for increased school funding.

Ideally, what you charge for tickets should be enough to cover production costs. However, if you depend solely on box office receipts to cover expenses, you may drive ticket prices too high, resulting in a low performance attendance. Keep the price reasonable. To determine what is reasonable, conduct a survey and check what the schools in the surrounding communities are charging for their public productions. If your school charges admission to football games, dances or other social events, see how your pricing compares with the price of admission to such events. Or consider charging half

the price of a local movie ticket, or the same prices charged
by local community theaters. Base the ticket price on what
the market will bear.

When production expenses run high, extra money can be
raised through program ads. Approach local lodge groups
like the Elks, Rotarians, Moose, Masons, Rebeccas, Odd
Fellows, and the Knights of Columbus; or try the Jaycees and
Kiwanis clubs; local veterans organizations; and local businesses catering to young people, such as restaurants, pizza
parlors, and clothing, sporting, and video or record stores.
Also ask cast and crew members if they have parents con-
nected to businesses they'd like to see advertised. For those
not interested in buying ad space, include Patron and Sponsor
sections for individual contributors.

What you charge for ads will depend on standard printing
and layout costs set by the printer. But if you and your
students do the layout work, you can set your own prices.
The following list gives a general idea of the type of ads you
can offer as well as a *reasonable* price scale for secondary
level productions:

Quarter page:	$25.00
Half page:	$45.00
Full page:	$75.00
Patron:	$10.00
Sponsor:	$20.00 or more

One reminder: Before soliciting ads, keep in mind that
the student(s) in charge of the program will need sufficient
time to type and lay out the ads for printing. Determine the
printer's timetable and establish firm deadlines. Once the
program goes to press, last-minute changes or additions can
be typed and mimeographed separately and included as an
insert.

Additional money can also be raised through fund-raising activities. Have the cast and crew (or drama club) organize a car wash or bake sale. Consider holding a raffle or an auction. I taught in one school where students auctioned off a list of services, such as tutoring, providing rides to school, carrying students' books between classes, cleaning students' lockers, or preparing a home-cooked ethnic meal. The possibilities are endless. When given a chance, students always come up with clever ideas and fund-raising strategies.

Finally, as opening night approaches, one big question is: "When should tickets go on sale?" A large part of your audience will be friends and relatives of your company, so make tickets available to cast and crew members at least two or three weeks in advance. However, promoting ticket sales within the school *too far* in advance often proves disappointing. Students rarely get excited about school functions or events until they are about to happen. Something that is not occurring or about to occur will not generate real enthusiasm or focused interest.

The big push for ticket sales should be during production week. Announce when and where tickets will be sold on the school's daily bulletin. If you want tickets to really sell, don't wait for students to show up at the box office *after* school; promote ticket sales *during* school.

The best time and place is the school cafeteria during lunch periods. Lunchtime is the only part of the day when students converge and socialize as a group during school hours. Use this time to promote your show. Have cast members dress in costumes; set up a table display with posters and balloons; use whatever gimmick will draw attention to the show and sell tickets.

16

Producing the High School Musical

Producing a high school musical is a challenging and unique experience often plagued with production headaches and added requirements that could easily overwhelm the best of drama teachers. Understanding the basic requirements and knowing how to fulfill them is the key. Before attempting a full-scale musical, it is well worth asking the following questions:

▶ **Question 1: WHAT AM I GETTING MYSELF INTO?**

There are greater technical demands in a musical than in a straight play. Its typical large cast requires a large number of uniform costumes and props for production numbers. Frequent mood changes may require additional lighting for special effects, such as follow spots, foot lights, and specials. In addition, the fast pacing of a musical requires any number of scrims, backdrops, and movable set pieces for quick scene changes. These frequent set and lighting changes create a heavy cue load. To meet all these technical demands, you will need a large, well-coordinated backstage crew, along with adequate stage facilities.

To produce a full-scale musical on a proscenium stage, there should be room for tormentors (or returns) to mask offstage areas, and ample wing and fly space to hold scenery. The stage area must be large enough for stage hands to move props and sets quickly between scenes without colliding with

Large-scale musicals require stage depth as well as ample wing and fly space to accommodate elaborate sets and large numbers of backdrops. "My Fair Lady," for example, required four sets, six backdrops, and seven unit pieces.

performers entering and exiting. If the theater or auditorium isn't acoustically sound, it should be wired with overhead mikes so actors can be heard clearly over the music. Remember, nothing is more deadly to a musical's success than actors drowned out by an orchestra.

▶ **Question 2: HOW DO I COORDINATE A MUSICAL STAFF AND ORCHESTRA?**

Ideally, the high school musical is produced with the cooperation of the music department. However, the talent and ability of music teachers and students, as well as their willingness to become involved, varies from school to school. If your situation is less than ideal, be prepared to hire a musical director and musicians. This is where funds from a program ad campaign come in handy.

If you do need to hire outside help, check with the music teacher for leads. Contact local and surrounding community theater and church choir groups for names of directors and accompanists. Also check the music and drama departments of local colleges, as well as music schools and conservatories, where students are always looking for work.

A *qualified* piano accompanist is essential. You cannot produce a musical without one. The most vital member of the music staff, the accompanist holds the rehearsal process together by providing accompaniment for musical numbers and dance music for the choreographer. He also helps the director pace and tie together scenes and musical numbers during run-throughs. In many circumstances, he serves as musical director. If qualified, he can teach the actors and chorus the show tunes, and when using a small orchestra, he can lead and cue musicians during performances.

Unless you have a background in dance, a choreographer will also be needed to stage production numbers. Hopefully a student or member of the faculty will be adequately trained to handle the position. If not, contact local studios and college dance departments as well as community theaters in your area.

▶ **Question 3: WHAT DO I NEED FOR AN ORCHESTRA?**

Piano and percussion alone are adequate to accompany a musical. To create a richer sound, a small, workable orchestra need only include one horn instrument (trumpet), one brass instrument (trombone), and one or two woodwind instruments (flute or piccolo, oboe or clarinet). Some publishers have special instrumental arrangements available for band and combo as well. One suggestion: look for musicians trained in more than one instrument to add variety to different parts of the score.

▶ Question 4: HOW CAN I GET MORE STUDENTS INTERESTED IN MUSICALS?

Consider creating a course or teaching a six- to eight-week unit in "Musical Theater Performance." To teach the basics of lyric interpretation, combine classes and team teach with the music or chorus teacher, or find a student to accompany your class or record a few show tunes for students to work on. Since most songs in a musical are an extension of dialogue and action, students will learn to use the same acting techniques required for a straight play. Begin by having students memorize and interpret the lyrics as a monologue, and then have them learn the melody. Once they've mastered the text and music, have them incorporate gestures, staging, or choreography. Wrap up the course by having students perform their musical numbers on stage using props and costumes. This type of course is not only fun, but a great way to expose students to musical theater.

(See Karen M. Hall's "Performing for the Musical Theatre," pp. 3–4; which provides detailed information on how to develop an effective musical theater course or unit.)

▶ Question 5: HOW DO I PREPARE STUDENTS FOR A MUSICAL AUDITION?

Although scripts should always be made available to students prior to auditions, bear in mind that companies holding rights to musicals often provide, as part of a package, only two copies of the *complete* libretto (one for the director and one for the stage manager), and only sides (smaller scripts containing one character's lines only) for actors. Acquiring additional copies may prove too costly.

When libretto copies are in limited supply, make sure students are given enough information to select and prepare for specific parts. Provide a brief synopsis of the musical, and a character sketch of all major and minor roles, as well as audition requirements for each. In addition, have copies of the musical album, tape, or CD available so students can familiarize themselves with the score. Or consider renting rehearsal tapes from the musical publisher. *Side One: Instrumental and Vocal* can be used to teach the students the songs, and *Side Two: Instrumental Only* can be used for rehearsals or in some cases for performance purposes. These tapes, which are in the same key as the orchestration, are note perfect and demonstrate the correct tempo for each song.

▶ **Question 6: HOW SHOULD A MUSICAL AUDITION BE HANDLED?**

Audition procedures need to be altered and expanded to accommodate dance and vocal auditions. Unless you're personally conducting dance auditions, provide a separate area for the choreographer to hold tryouts. Have the musical director (and/or accompanist) sit in with you on auditions. Combining vocal auditions with character readings will provide a better picture of students' vocal potential and suitability for roles.

If for some reason a musical director cannot be scheduled for auditions, handle the vocal auditions yourself. My procedure is simple. Students auditioning for lead roles are required to prepare a song from the show. This accomplishes three things: it gives students a taste of what a professional audition is like; it gives *me* a better idea of their range and how well they can handle the score; and it also indicates how serious students are about becoming involved. Any student wanting a major part, but unwilling to prepare adequately for tryouts, will usually not be committed to the time and work a musical requires.

If you don't have an accompanist or a rehearsal tape, you can evaluate your students' vocal ability by having those auditioning for *leads* sing along with the original Broadway album or tape. Don't worry, the voice on the recording will not drown out the auditioning student's voice if you use a portable record or cassette player with small speakers.

Students auditioning for *chorus parts* can sing a song of their choice either with accompaniment (recorded music), or a cappella. Allow those too frightened to sing alone to audition with someone else. More students will try out when permitted to sing as part of a duet or trio. The grouping is also small enough to allow evaluation of each voice. Making these allowances encourages students to support one another on stage and eases audition tensions, especially when trying out is a new experience.

Keeping musical auditions open is crucial, for it allows students to see how well others perform and gives the inexperienced students something to strive for. In addition, it is good publicity for the show.

Musical tryouts can be long and tedious; don't let them run *too* late in the afternoon or evening. Remember, you are dealing with adolescents who have schoolwork and concerned parents waiting at home. If necessary, schedule an additional day.

THE MUSICAL AUDITION SHEET

The audition sheet should provide you with: a) the specific parts students are interested in trying out for, and b) a clear picture of a student's preparedness, specific talents, and musical experience. Include the following questions:

- Have you prepared a song?
- Have you prepared a song from the show? If so, what?
- Will you accept a chorus part? Singing or dancing?
- Have you had any voice or dance training? If so, list schools or instructors.
- Have you ever been in a musical? If yes, list shows and parts.

There are no hard-and-fast rules on how to handle a musical audition. The goal is to develop auditioning procedures that will best help you determine in the shortest amount of time, a student's potential talent, special abilities, and attitude regarding full commitment to the show.

REHEARSAL SCHEDULING TIPS

Whereas a straight play can be mounted in six to eight weeks, a high school musical will need a minimum of twelve, with well-coordinated scheduling. Usually additional space will be needed for rehearsals and set construction. The use of class-rooms and larger facilities, such as the gym or cafeteria, should always be coordinated and cleared *in advance* with the front office and with the appropriate school departments.

If rehearsal or construction space is limited, work out necessary production details and scheduling alternatives first, and give yourself enough scheduling leeway to meet production deadlines. It's better to have extra time than not enough.

To take full advantage of after-school time, have vocal, dance, and staging rehearsals scheduled every day. Provide a copy of the score to your accompanist as early as possible. Have him learn and record the music for the dance numbers immediately so that vocal and dance rehearsals can be held simultaneously. This provides greater scheduling flexibility. Once dance numbers are choreographed and learned, select a

A small school auditorium can be used to advantage with fragmentary sets and unit pieces in musicals such as "Gypsy" and "Dames at Sea." This kind of production design keeps costs down, takes less time, and makes it possible to mount a musical more easily.

student dance captain to lead rehearsals whenever the choreographer is not present.

One reminder: Although students may have prepared a song for auditions using the original recording, the Broadway album or tape should *not* be used to teach the songs and dance numbers for the actual production. Most recordings differ in tempo and length from the standard score. You'll only confuse actors and dancers and waste precious rehearsal time. Use only music taped from the actual score by your accompanist or from a rented rehearsal tape.

To meet production deadlines, have set construction work going on daily. Assign production work to actors when they're not needed on stage. When crew heads who have parts in the show are called to rehearsal, they should select a crew member to stand second in command so that production work continues uninterrupted and momentum is maintained.

Production week is an especially critical time for a musical. Technical elements must be pulled together: cues need to be coordinated; set and costume changes have to be timed perfectly; and costumes often need last-minute adjustments. Add the orchestra, and you will often find students overwhelmed. Therefore schedule as many rehearsals with the orchestra as possible to adjust tempos and balance vocals.

THE LAST WORD

Every teacher is different. Every teaching situation is different. All teachers have strengths. All teachers have weaknesses. Some may be stronger in certain areas of theater than others—some in stagecraft and technical theater, others in dramatic literature and theater history, and still others in stage direction, choreography, or design. But no matter what your personal strengths and weaknesses, never, *ever* doubt your talents or your ability to learn.

More important, never allow your shortcomings to discourage or prevent you from exposing students to the full production experience. Play production requires many areas of skill; you can't be an expert in all of them. Seek help and support wherever needed. If necessary, find a carpenter, a seamstress, a lighting technician, or anyone else to help teach students. Use one of the recommended production handbooks to see you through the rough spots. As your confidence increases, so too will your skills.

Experience, whether good or bad, is your ultimate teacher.

~~GOOD LUCK.~~

Break a leg!

APPENDIXES

1

Sample Course Outlines

This appendix contains sample course outlines of the type you will need to submit to your school's administration as part of a course of study. They can also be used as course synopses to be given to students at the beginning of a term. How you design your own courses will naturally depend on the type of teaching position you hold, as well as the individual needs of your students. These sample outlines can be used as a starting point.

For more information about designing courses see chapter 5 of this book. You might also wish to consult Charlotte Kay Motter, *Theatre in High School: Planning, Teaching, Directing.*

Sample Outline for a High School Play Production Course

The object of Drama I is to make the student aware of theater as a craft. The student will be exposed to the various practical elements needed to put on a play, and will learn the duties and roles of the personnel needed for a successful production.

The following production elements will be covered in depth:

1. Production staff and its functions
2. Stage terminology
3. Styles of production
4. Types of sets
5. Set construction
6. Lighting
7. History of the physical theater and its relationship to the development of drama
8. The basic structure of a play
9. Styles and forms of drama and representative plays
10. Musical theater

In order to put into practice what is learned in the classroom, each student must put in, during the course of the *entire school year*, 30 crew hours working in some technical capacity (other than acting) on a drama department public production. Anyone who completes *over* 30 crew hours by the end of the school year will receive extra points towards his or her final grade for the year.

The Drama I student should learn the proper skills, if he or she is to participate effectively in the drama department's major productions.

Sample Outline for a High School Acting Course

Drama II is primarily set up as an actor's workshop. It is an acting-oriented course in which each student is given the opportunity to develop various skills which include:

1. Body development and control through dance and yoga exercises
2. Relaxation
3. Concentration
4. Improvisation
5. Pantomime
7. The acting techniques of Stanislavski and Meyerhold
8. Extensive scene work and assignments
9. Study of the styles and forms of drama and how they relate to the actor
10. Basic makeup techniques

Due to the nature of the course, students are required to wear pants and soft-soled shoes to class. Lack of conformity to this rule will result in the student's exclusion from the day's workshop activity—and, therefore, a zero for the day. Class participation and the completion of acting assignments are essential if a student is to gain anything from this type of course.

Drama II students are also required to write one production review per semester as part of the course work. This will help the student become more aware of the various production elements with which the actor must constantly work.

Sample Outline for a High School
Theater Design Course

Drama III is designed to help the advanced drama student develop skills in scenic, costume, and lighting design. The course will also cover the various styles of production and how they relate to the elements and principles of design. Basic elements of directing in terms of overall unity in production will also be discussed.

The Drama III student is expected to be continually at work on projects during the first semester. The basis for grading in the course will be four major projects:

1. Designing a backdrop for a musical
2. Constructing a box set model of a play
3. Designing costumes for a character from a musical or play
4. Designing a lighting plot for a musical or play

As a final project, each student is required by the end of the school year to complete a production book on a play or musical of their choice. This project includes:

1. An in-depth play and character analysis
2. An overall design concept for the play
3. A complete set of costume, lighting, and set design renderings
4. A set of floor plans with furniture and props

Sample Outline for a Self-Directed Drama Course

Drama IV is geared to give the advanced drama student the opportunity to pursue intensively and largely independently those areas of the performing arts that are of special interest to him or her, such as stage and film directing, play writing, filmmaking, or a specialized area of design. Each student must produce material that lives up to both qualitative and quantitative standards. Four major projects will serve as the basis for grading in the course.

The following is a list of possible projects. This list is merely suggestive and is by no means to be considered inclusive.

1. Write an original skit or one-act play.
2. Write and direct a video short.
3. Write an adaptation of a short story, cartoon, folk tale, etc., for the stage.
4. Write an original script for a puppet play.
5. Design and build puppets.
6. Produce a puppet show for the lower elementary grades.
7. Cast and direct a scene or one-act play.
8. Design and construct the costume and makeup of a science fiction or animated character.

2

Sample Outline for Student Production Reviews

Every drama teacher should encourage students to see plays. When possible, organize field trips to professional performances. Group discounts for matinees can be arranged with the theater, and if necessary students can do fund-raising activities to cover the cost of admission. Students should also be encouraged to see college and community theater productions, as well as other high school productions. Exposure to live theater greatly enriches the school curriculum.

Sample Outline for Student Production Reviews

Each drama student is required to submit *one* production review of a live performance *every quarter*. Make this a carefully thought-out critique in essay form. Sloppy or rushed work will be returned as unacceptable. Minimum of 500 words. *Extra credit* for typewritten work. The following elements must be included:

A. Name of the play. Give date seen and where.
B. Name of amateur theater group or professional company.
C. Note the director, leading actors, and any pertinent production people or particulars.
D. Note the type of theater seen (tragedy, melodrama, comedy, musical, etc.), and the play's setting and time period.
E. Briefly describe the plot.
F. Discuss in detail as many elements of the production as you can. Carefully explain why or why not you believe something worked for the director. If possible, discuss all of the following:
    1. Directing (everything points to the director)
    2. Acting
    3. Music
    4. Singing and dancing (for musicals)
    5. Costumes
    6. Sets (were they appropriate, inventive, realistic?)
    7. Type of set(s) (cyclorama, box set, curtains, fragmentary set, backdrops, etc.)
    8. Lighting (how effective or ineffective was it in creating the proper mood and atmosphere)
    9. Sound effects
    10. Audience reaction

Be sure your name, course number, and the title of the production reviewed appear on the first page of your review.

3

Sample Student Scene Critique Sheet

Scene critique sheets are an invaluable learning tool, for they help students develop their critical faculties and increase their powers of observation.

Sample Student Scene Critique Sheet

Name: _____ Date: _____ Class: _____

Play and author: _____

Actor #1: _____ in the role of _____

Actor #2: _____ in the role of _____

After the performance, answer the following questions indicating strengths and areas needing improvement.

1. Where and when did the scene take place?

2. Who were the characters?

3. Did the characters accurately reflect the social background and period of the play?

4. Did the actors succeed in immersing themselves in the characters or were they playing themselves?

5. What was the relationship of the characters to one another?

6. What did each character want?

7. Did each character reach his objective?

8. What gestures, movements, or stage business did each character use to express inner thoughts or feelings? Was it convincing?

9. While watching the scene, did the characters arouse any feelings in you, such as sympathy, disgust, hatred, affection, amusement, etc.?

10. Comment briefly on each actor's performance in terms of the following acting elements: concentration, stage presence, voice and diction.

4

Building and Covering a Flat

Building a stock of reusable scenery is an essential part of any school drama program. It all begins with the basic flat which when combined with other flats forms the "walls" of the onstage set. This appendix includes a list of the tools, materials, and stage hardware needed to build and cover a permanent flat as well as an easy-to-follow assembly guide to help get you started. Tools and materials can be purchased at any hardware store or lumberyard.

Basic Parts of a Plain Flat

Two stiles (vertical side pieces)

Two rails (top and bottom crosspieces)

One toggle rail (cross member located between two end rails)

Four corner blocks (reinforcing triangles)

Two corner braces (diagonal braces used to keep frame from buckling)

Keystones (rectangles used to reinforce joints between toggle rail and stiles as well as cross members and corner braces.

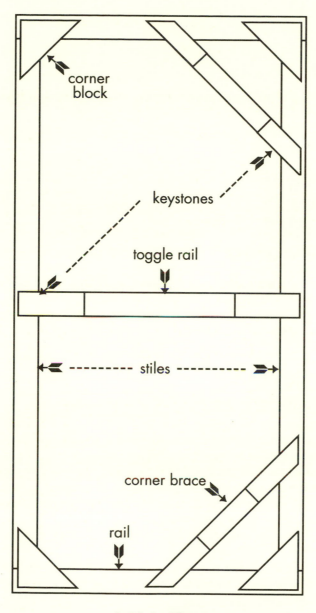

corner
block

keystones

toggle rail

stiles

corner brace

rail

A Plain Flat

Step One: Build the Frame

TOOLS

- Crosscut hand saw or power circular saw with crosscut blade
- Framing square
- Measuring tape
- Rip or claw hammer

MATERIALS

- Top grade 1 × 3 inch stock of white pine or spruce
- No. 5 (⅝ inch) corrugators

SPECIFICATIONS

- Standard widths of flats vary from 1 to 6 feet; standard heights of flats vary from 9 to 12 feet.
- Joints are butt joints and assembled with ⅝ inch corrugators.
- Rails, toggle rail, stiles, and corner braces are made of 1 × 3 inch stock.

INSTRUCTIONS

1. Determine the required height and width of flat.
2. Measure and cut stiles (vertical pieces) to the desired length and cut the rails (top and bottom pieces) to the desired width. Remember that because the stiles fit within the rails, you need to consider the combined width of the rails in your height measurements.
3. Cut the toggle rail (center piece) to the desired width *minus* the combined width of the two stiles.
4. Measure and cut corner braces to fit at a 45 degree angle between the stiles and rail.
5. Lay out all of the pieces and abut all of the joints. Use the framing square to ensure that all outside joints are perpendicular to each other.
6. Assemble using No. 5 corrugators.

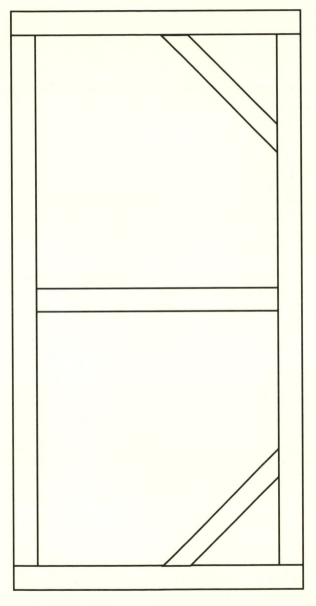

Step One: Build the Frame

Step Two: Add Corner Blocks and Keystones

TOOLS

- Crosscut hand saw or power circular saw with a fine-tooth plywood blade
- Framing square
- Hammer

MATERIALS

- Plywood (¼ inch)
- Clout nails (1¼ inch)

SPECIFICATIONS

- Cut keystones with the outside grain of plywood running on the long dimension.
- Drive all nails "home" and clinch on the opposite side of the flat.

INSTRUCTIONS

1. Corner blocks: cut two 10 × 10 inch plywood squares, and then cut them in half diagonally from corner to corner, making four triangles.
2. Keystones: cut six 2½ × 8 inch plywood pieces to reinforce joints of cross members and corner braces. These can be angled to fit.
3. Place corner blocks and keystones ¾ inch from the outside edge of stiles and rails. Nail in place using clout nails. (See diagram of Step Two for placement of nails.)

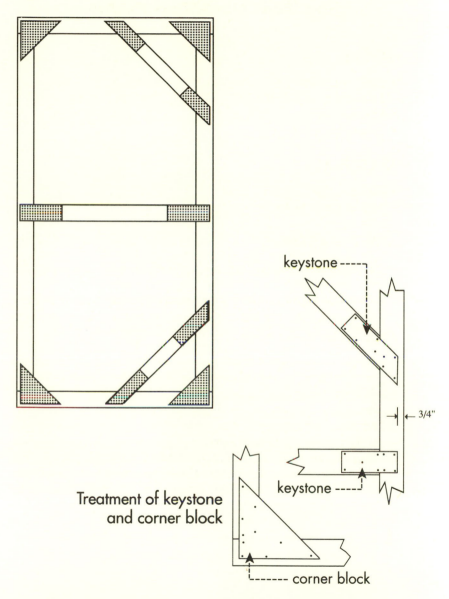

keystone -----

← 3/4"

keystone -----

Treatment of keystone
and corner block

-------- corner block

Step Two: Add Corner Blocks and Keystones

Step Three: Attach Stage Hardware

TOOLS

- Measuring tape
- Hand or electric drill with ⅜ inch bit
- Screwdriver
- X-acto knife

MATERIALS

- No. 8 (¾ inch) wood screws
- Sash cord (¼ inch)

STAGE HARDWARE

- One brace cleat (metal plate used to hold a stage brace hook)
- Two lash cleats
- Two tie-off cleats (Lash and tie-off cleats are used for mounting and joining flats; for instructions on mounting and joining flats see Warren C. Lounsbury's *Theatre Backstage from A to Z*).

INSTRUCTIONS

1. Position *brace cleat* approximately two thirds of the height of the flat on the back of the right stile. Attach with ¾ inch wood screws.
2. If flats are to be lashed together, lash and tie-off cleats should also be mounted. Position the first *lash cleat* below the top left corner block, and the second above the toggle rail on the left stile. Position one *tie-off cleat* on each stile 30 to 36 inches from the floor at a slight angle to the stile.
3. Drill a ⅜ inch hole in the top right corner block.
4. Knot one end of the sash cord and run it through the hole; using the X-acto knife, cut cord the length of the flat.

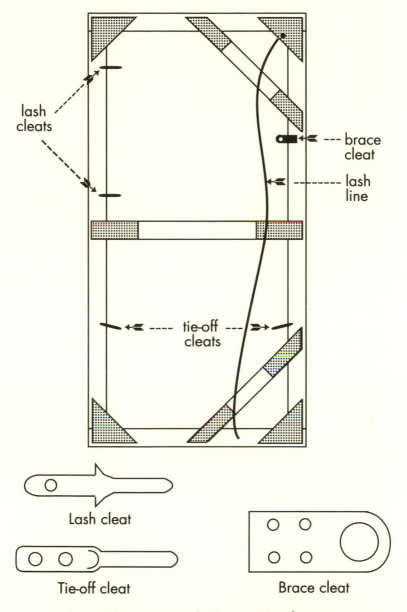

lash
cleats

brace
cleat

lash
line

tie-off
cleats

Lash cleat

Tie-off cleat

Brace cleat

Step Three: Attach Stage Hardware

Step Four: Cover Flat with Muslin

TOOLS

- Measuring tape
- Scissors
- Staple gun
- Single-edged razor blade

MATERIALS

- Role of 81-inch-wide heavy (128 to 140 threads per square inch) muslin sheeting
- Staples (¼ inch)

SPECIFICATIONS

- When attaching muslin to flat, staples should be placed one inch apart along the edge of stiles and rails.

INSTRUCTIONS

1. Lay flat face-up on a work surface.
2. Be sure there are no unclinched nails on the rails, stiles, or toggle rail to snag, puncture, or rip the muslin.
3. Measure and cut the muslin the length and width of the flat *plus* 3 inches total.
4. Draw the cloth across the face of the frame with the edge of the material flush with the top rail edge; staple the muslin to the far edge corner (first staple).
5. Stretch the muslin across the width of the frame and staple it to the opposite far edge corner of the top rail (second staple).
6. Stretch the muslin lengthwise and staple it to the far edge corners of the bottom rail (third and fourth staples). These four preliminary staples set up the initial tension and can be easily removed if more tension is required to create a smooth surface across and down the length of the stiles.
7. Continue to stretch and staple the material along the edge of each stile.

8. Staple the muslin across the edge of the top rail, then give it one last stretch and staple it along the edge of the bottom rail.
9. Finishing options: With a single-edged razor blade, trim the surplus material flush to the edges of the flat using your thumb as a guide; or, wrap and staple the surplus cloth every six inches on the back surface of the stiles and bottom rail.

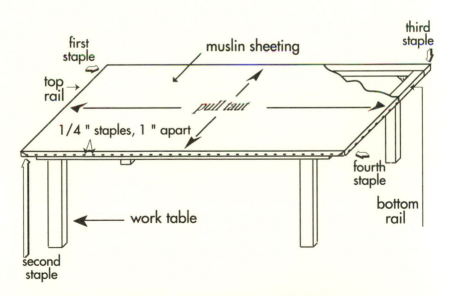

Step Four: Cover Flat with Muslin

5

Rules Regarding Educational Use of Literary Works

Any drama teacher who intends to reproduce and distribute theater material and plays for classroom use should be aware of the following rules in order to avoid copyright infringement.

Rules Regarding Educational Use of Literary Works

(Reprinted by permission of The MIT Press, publisher, from *The Copyright Book: A Practical Guide*, 3d edition, copyright © 1990 William S. Strong, pp. 147–151.)

I. SINGLE COPYING FOR TEACHERS

A single copy may be made of any of the following by or for a teacher at his or her individual request for his or her scholarly research or use in teaching or preparation to teach a class:

- A. A chapter from a book;
- B. An article from a periodical or newspaper;
- C. A short story, short essay, or short work;
- D. A chart, graph, diagram, drawing, cartoon, or picture from a book, periodical, or newspaper.

II. MULTIPLE COPIES FOR CLASSROOM USE

Multiple copies (not to exceed in any event more than one copy per pupil in a course) may be made by or for the teacher giving the course for classroom use or discussion, provided that

A. The copying meets the tests of brevity and spontaneity as defined below, and
B. Meets the cumulative effect test as defined below, and
C. Each copy includes a notice of copyright.

DEFINITIONS

Brevity
- (i) Poetry
  - (a) A complete poem if less than 250 words and if printed on not more than two pages or,
  - (b) From a longer poem, an excerpt of not more than 250 words.
- (ii) Prose
  - (a) Either a complete article, story, or essay of less than 2,500 words or
  - (b) An excerpt from any prose work of not more than 1,000 words or 10 percent of the work, whichever is less, but in any event a minimum of 500 words.

[Each of the numerical limits stated in "i" and "ii" above may be expanded to permit the completion of an unfinished line of a poem or an unfinished prose paragraph.]

- (iii) Illustration

  One chart, graph, diagram, drawing, cartoon, or picture per book or per periodical issue.
- (iv) "Special" works

  Certain works in poetry, prose, or in poetic prose which often combine language with illustrations and which are intended sometimes for children and at other times for a more general audience fall short of 2,500 words in their entirety. Paragraph "ii" above notwithstanding, such "special works" may not be reproduced in their entirety; however, an excerpt comprising not more than two of the published pages of such special works and containing not more than 10 percent of the words found in the text thereof may be reproduced.

Spontaneity

(i) The copying is at the instance and inspiration of the individual.

(ii) The inspiration and decision to use the work and the moment of its use for maximum teaching effectiveness are so close in time that it would be unreasonable to expect a timely reply to a request for permission.

Cumulative Effect

(i) The copying of the material is for only one course in the school in which the copies are made.

(ii) Not more than one short poem, article, story, essay, or two excerpts may be copied from the same author, nor more than three from the same collective work or periodical volume during one class term.

(iii) There shall not be more than nine instances of such multiple copying for one course during one class term.

[The limitations stated in "ii" and "iii" above shall not apply to current news periodicals and newspapers and current news sections of other periodicals.]

III. PROHIBITIONS AS TO I AND II ABOVE

Notwithstanding any of the above, the following shall be prohibited:

A. Copying shall not be used to create or to replace or substitute for anthologies, compilations, or collective works. Such replacement or substitution may occur whether copies of various works or excerpts therefrom are accumulated or reproduced and used separately.

B. There shall be no copying of or from works intended to be "consumable" in the course of study or of teaching. These include workbooks, exercises, standardized tests, and test booklets and answer sheets and like consumable material.

C. Copying shall not
   (a) Substitute for the purchase of books, publishers' reprints, or periodicals;
   (b) Be directed by higher authority; or
   (c) Be repeated with respect to the same item by the same teacher from term to term.

D. No charge shall be made to the student beyond the actual cost of the photocopying.

William S. Strong goes on to further explain:

. . . If copying for classroom use stays within these guidelines, it will without question be considered fair use. It is conceivable that in a given case a substantial departure from the guidelines might also be considered fair use, by application of the four basic statutory criteria.

Where an anticipated use falls outside the boundaries drawn by the guidelines, it is advisable to seek permission of the copyright owner. One way of doing this is to write directly to whoever is named in the copyright notice on the work. There will of course be works for which no copyright owner is clearly designated. For example, the copyright may be given in the name of a publisher that has gone out of business, or you may be working from a reprinted excerpt that does not bear copyright notice. In any case, unless it is appropriate to write to the publisher, you should write to the Copyright Office to request information regarding the copyright owners. If the Copyright Office is unable to provide guidance, it is likely that reproducing the work would be considered reasonable under the circumstances.

In general, publishers and authors are fairly accommodating in granting permission for educational uses of their works. However, that permission must be explicit. One is not entitled to rely on silence.

"Spontaneity" is a difficult quality to prove or disprove. However, your credibility will decrease, and your liability will increase, if the photocopying that you authorize begins to assume a pattern or if photocopying is "spontaneously" authorized for works that ordinarily would be considered obvious parts of the curriculum.

The requirement that each copy reproduced for classroom use include a notice of copyright should be strictly complied with. Where you are taking an excerpt from a work in such a way that the copyright notice included in the work will not be reproduced, it is your responsibility to ensure that copyright notice in the proper form is put on each copy reproduced. This notice should be identical to that on the work itself. If you are reproducing a previously unpublished work—for example, a friend's manuscript—be certain to obtain his permission for publication. You should put on it proper notice or a legend such as I have suggested for limited publications: *This copy is for private circulation only and may not be used or distributed in any other manner.* To be safer yet, you might require that each copy be returned to you at the end of the term.

The guidelines purport to cover single copying for a teacher's personal use. In my opinion they are probably too narrow in this respect. However, copying for personal use must be distinguished from copying in the course of business, and "business" includes teaching duties.

It is important to remember that these guidelines expressly forbid the making of anthologies composed of periodicals and books, even though these may be sold to students at or below cost. They also forbid the copying of consumable items such as workbooks, standardized tests, and answer sheets. Although some flexibility may exist in other parts of the guidelines, it is doubtful that any court would sanction much deviation in either of these respects.

Finally, these guidelines do not apply to sheet music or to off-the-air taping of broadcasts. A teacher should seek administrative permission for any activity of this type.

6

Recommended Plays for Junior High School

This appendix contains a list of plays and musicals with mature themes and challenging roles for twelve- to fifteen-year-olds.

Key to Publishers (see appendix 8 for publishers' addresses):

> AP: Anchorage Press
> Baker: Baker's Plays
> DPC: Dramatic Publishing Company
> FP: The Freelance Press
> French: Samuel French

The Arkansaw Bear.   Aurand Harris.   Drama.
Flexible cast of 6.   1 set.   (AP)

Upset by her grandfather's impending death, Tish finds herself in a world of fantasy created by her wishing on a star while at her "special tree." There she meets the World's Greatest Dancing Bear. He is old like her grandfather, and running away from death. In trying to help him, she begins to understand the meaning of life and death, which helps her cope with her sadness.

The Boy Who Stole the Stars.   Julian Wiles.   Drama.
2 males, 2 females, 1 dragon.   1 exterior.   (DPC)

A young boy discovers his grandfather is dying. The old man's behavior has changed; he is now short-tempered and has stopped telling his wonderful stories. In order to return him to his former self, the boy enlists his grandfather's help on a school project—counting the stars. The old man's interest is renewed, and he tells the boy the story of the dragon in the sky. The dragon, he explains, is there to guard the stars, for should they return to earth, there would be a new paradise with no unhappiness or death. Hearing this, the boy goes up into the sky to slay the dragon and return the stars to earth as a way of keeping his grandfather alive. By the end of the play, the boy realizes how much his grandfather loves him. "I don't need to live forever," says the old man, "I need you to care about me."

Cheaper by the Dozen. Dramatized by Christopher Sergel. Based on the novel by Frank Gilbreth and Ernestine Gilbreth Carey. Drama.
9 males, 7 females. 1 interior. (DPC)

This is the story of a funny, resourceful, and unorthodox father who takes every opportunity to organize his large and delightful family into a more efficient household. While this provides uproarious humor, there is a pressing reason that underlies his behavior—a heart condition which he is keeping secret. The girls can't understand their father's behavior, and neither does he understand theirs. Anne, the oldest, rebels against her father, making them both miserable. In a deft and moving scene, Dad finally comes to the realization that Anne has now grown up.

Dags. Debra Oswald. Comedy.
4 males, 6 females, extras. Area staging. (DPC)

Gillian is a "dag"—a nerd, a misfit, who doesn't think much of herself. She takes us on an excruciating roller coaster ride through the anguished and awkward world of adolescence. It isn't easy coping with her beautiful, bouncy, popular sister and her gossipy girlfriends, as she desperately tries to be beautiful and popular. Gillian feels pushed to the limit after a mad crush on the school's biggest hunk and a blind date with a mega-dag. In the end, she reaches a turning point and triumphs in an exhilarating moment of self-confidence and awareness.

Doors.   Susan L. Zeder.   Drama.
3 males, 1 female.   1 set.   (AP)

This is the story of Jeffrey, a twelve-year-old boy who is trying to come to grips with his parents' impending divorce. He confronts and plays out his fears and fantasies with his best friend, Sandy. Once the issue is in the open, the whole family can begin to heal. The play emphasizes the importance of talking and listening.

Escape to Freedom.   Ossie Davis.   Drama.
3 black males, 1 black female, 2 white males, 1 white female.   Multiple sets.   (Baker)

This biographical play is about the boyhood of Frederick Douglass, who was born a slave and later in life became an abolitionist and orator. To illustrate the importance of education, the story centers on Fred's struggle to learn to read— his ticket to a better life. In time he attains his freedom and runs away disguised as a free sailor.

The Everyday Adventures of Harriet Handelman (Super Genius).   Greg Atkins.   Comedy.
9 males, 4 females, extras.   Simple sets (set and prop design sketches included).   (Baker)

When a mysterious Shadowy Figure steals a class science project, the brilliant Harriet Handelman is called upon to save the day. Harriet, her friends, and CIA agent Terry Alexander pursue the villain's trail, which leads them to many exotic places. Harriet ingeniously saves the world by inventing "re-wind time" that sends everyone backwards through the play in a hilarious scene. The play is jam-packed with chase scenes, sight gags, a few brushes with death, and enough gadgets and zany gismos to satisfy even James Bond.

Fame.   Adapted for the stage by Christopher Sergel.   Based on the screenplay by Christopher Gore.   Drama.
9 males, 15 females, extras as desired.
Area staging.   (DPC)

At the opening of the play, we find the New York City School for Performing Arts in the midst of auditioning students. There are young people from every walk of life who have nothing in common but one dream — and we see each of them pursue it in their own way. We watch as they learn to work through their own special problems. There's Doris, pushed and prodded by her persistent stage mother; Montgomery, lonely and in need of a friend; Ralph, intense and angry with everyone; Coco, too big for her britches; Bruno, musically talented but stifled by a bad "attitude"; and Leroy from the ghetto, a scholastic disaster, but a brilliant dancer. We watch as they interact with each other and with their teachers to create an exciting theatrical event.

Friday's Child.   Pamela Sterling.   Drama.
6 males, 2 females.   Area staging.   (DPC)

The play revolves around the coming of age of Tom, a thirteen-year-old boy in Northern Ireland. He is torn between thoughts of killing an enemy to prove his manhood or following his conscience to aid a victim of the war. The decisions he must make are difficult ones. On one side, his grandfather fills his head with stories and ballads of Irish warriors, his sixteen-year-old block captain tempts him to join the IRA and berates him for his childish indecisions, and British soldiers tease and provoke him. On the other side, his sister Meg begs him not to carry a weapon and become a target. But it is Tara who draws out his caring and humane instincts. Tom's inner struggle and torn loyalties become for him a desperate fight for his life.

The Indian Captive. Developed from history by Charlotte B. Chorpenning. Drama.
3 males, 3 females, 5 children. 2 sets. (AP)

Captured by Indians, a pioneer girl is taken to the camp of Chief Cornplanter. Her courage is severely tested but her spirit proves firm. Eventually she is adopted into the Seneca tribe and learns their ways and customs. They soon grow to love her dearly—so much so that when her mother comes for her, they disguise the girl and threaten to kill her mother if she reveals her identity. In a dramatic moment, Eleanor courageously keeps faith with the Seneca tribe while desperately longing to make a sign of love to her mother. The chief finally realizes that the young girl he has grown to love belongs with her own people, and he lets her go.

Johnny Tremain. Dramatized by Lola H. Jennings and Coleman A. Jennings. Based on the novel by Esther Forbes. Drama.
13 males, 2 females. Unit set. (DPC)

Johnny, a young apprentice silversmith, gets caught up in the stirring events that lead to the Boston Tea Party and the Battle of Lexington. A moving Revolutionary story filled with danger, courage, and intrigue, seen through the eyes of a young boy who, without the support of a family, is forced to make his way alone.

Little Women.   Dramatized by Sara Spencer.   Drama.
2 males, 10 females.   1 set.   (AP)

This faithful adaptation of Louisa May Alcott's story is built on the delightful adventures of the four March girls: the performance of the amateur play, the ongoing feud with Aunt March, the sacrifice of Jo's beautiful hair, Beth catching scarlet fever, and other wonderful episodes. This adaptation is well within the scope and understanding of the junior high age level.

Make a Friend, Find a Friend.   Paul Maar.   Translated by Anita and Alex Page.   Drama.
4 males, 3 females, or 3 males, 4 females.   Representational sets.   (Baker)

A boy with a need to have his own way creates a fantasy world that includes a fantasy companion. It is a place where he gets everything he wants and always wins at every game. The withdrawal into his imagination alienates his parents and anyone who could have been his friend. When the imaginary companion begins to take over his life, he realizes he must choose either to remain in his fantasy land, or to return to the real world where friends and family wait to accept him as he is.

The Man-Child.   Arnold Rabin.   Comedy/drama.
6 males, 4 females, 1 male non-speaking part.   Multiple interiors.   (Baker)

The road to manhood can be both difficult and funny. This is the story of the days preceding young Allen's Bar Mitzvah when everything that can go wrong does go wrong. There are complications when a lie turns the boy against his mother. This touching account of a young boy who becomes a man by conquering adversity is told in the narrative of the boy's wise old grandmother, Mrs. Wishnefsky.

The Medicine Show (or How to Succeed in Medicine without Really Trying). Virginia Glasgow Koste. An American version of Molière's *A Doctor in Spite of Himself.* Farce. Flexible cast of 8. Bare stage. (AP)

The infamous doctor engages in a variety of hilarious plots and counterplots as he psyches out everybody in sight. Fortunately by relying on his wits, he always lands happily on his feet.

Newcomer. Janet Thomas. Drama.
2 males, 3 females. Simple unit sets. (AP)

Mai Li, a refugee from Southeast Asia, suddenly finds herself in an American high school atmosphere, alienated by language and custom. Benny, a hip, all-American high school hero who is Chinese, is asked to communicate with her. Afraid of being ridiculed by his peers, he refuses. Both he and Mai Li are forced to confront their individual need for acceptance in a multiethnic community.

Night of the Pterodactyls. Julian Wiles. Comedy.
5 males, 5 females, extras. 1 exterior, 1 interior. (DPC)

Twelve-year-old Whit thinks Carly, a newcomer in town, is the ugliest girl who ever lived. She is also the smartest person he has ever met. Carly's obsession with dinosaurs leads to Whit's obsession with her — feelings he has trouble explaining to his secret, all-boy group of friends known as the Gross

Associates. When Carly digs up a nest of pterodactyl eggs in Mrs. Webster's rose garden, there is pandemonium. The National Guard is called in to keep away the curious. In a dramatic finale, the eggs are to be excavated on live television. But the glare of the TV lights is so bright that it warms the pterodactyl eggs . . . and something curious happens.

Noah and the Great Auk. Bix L. Doughty. Drama.
Flexible cast of 6. Unit set. (AP)

This contemporary version of Noah deals with endangered species. To protect her solitary egg for the future, an Auk makes an alliance with Noah on behalf of all the animals. There is a shipboard mutiny instigated by the Hyena, and the Auk sacrifices her life to save Noah and mankind. The rains have stopped and the survivors, with the precious Auk egg, debark onto a fragile world and an uncertain future—which is now the present.

Noodle Doodle Box. Paul Maar. Translated by Anita Page and Alex Page. Comedy/drama.
3 males, 3 females, or mixed cast. (Baker)

Two clowns named Pepper and Zacharias each possess a box/house/space which they refuse to share with each other. Suddenly a pretentious, overbearing Drum Major appears on the scene and decides he wants both boxes for himself. He pits Pepper and Zacharias against each other so he can steal the boxes. In the end, they magically acquire one new box, which they learn to share and enjoy together.

O Ye Jigs and Juleps! Adapted by Don Musselman. Based on the book by Virginia Cary Hudson. Comedy.
20 males, 23 females (with doubling, 12 males, 15 females). Unit set with inserts. (AP)

Virginia, a bright eleven-year-old, enjoys life in rural America. She delightfully charms the townspeople with her shrewd and ingenious comments on life, death, food, cattle, and mint juleps. Based on authentic essays by a child in the early 1900s, this play demonstrates what life was like in a small Kentucky town nearly a century ago.

One to Grow On.   Brian Kral.   Drama.
7 males, 1 female.   Multiple representational sets.   (AP)

This powerful biographical play is about a young man's twelfth birthday spent in the company of his widowed grandfather, and how they come to a deeper realization of what it means to have a family.

The Outing.   Arnold Rabin.   Drama.
5 males, 4 females, 1 non-speaking part.   Bare stage.   (AP)

Walter Newcombe is upset; he is always being picked on by his peers because his talents are different than theirs. His mother's efforts to help him put his feelings in perspective are thwarted by his father's expectations of him. The strained relations reach a crisis at the father's lodge picnic when Walter trips in a race. Rather than further disappoint his father, he refuses to participate in the other athletic events. At home, the family confronts the significance of the events at the outing, and by doing so, they begin to know themselves and what they mean to each other.

The Pin Balls.   Adapted by Aurand Harris.   Based on the novel by Betsy Byars.   Drama.
3 males, 2 females.   1 set.   (AP)

Three teenagers are bounced about like pinballs from one foster home to another. Fifteen-year-old Carlie, street-wise and a born leader, is a victim of child abuse. Thirteen-year-old Harvey is wheelchair-bound after his drunken father ran over both his legs with his car. Eight-year-old Thomas J. was abandoned as a baby. Each longs for the comfort of a home. Finally they all come together for the first time with Mrs. Mason, an encouraging and understanding foster mother. By the end of the summer the "pinballs" have become a "family."

The Ransom of Red Chief.   Adapted by Anne Coultier Martens.   Based on a story by O. Henry.   Comedy.
5 males, 9 females.   Simplified sets.   (DPC)

Bill and Sam bite off more than they can chew when they kidnap a brat known as "Red," who keeps his captors hopping. Sam tries to entertain Red—or Red Chief, as he prefers to be called—but finds it exhausting. Having lost all patience, Sam makes the mistake of getting Red mad. Red Chief's vengeance soon has Sam totally exasperated. Instead of receiving a hefty ransom, the two unfortunate criminals finally end up having to *pay* what little they have for the privilege of returning the so-called victim to his parents.

Song of the Navigator.   Michael Cowell.   Drama/comedy.
5 males, 2 females, with doubling.   Single sets.   (DPC)

Gabby, a teenage boy from Saipan, near Guam, attends school on another island. When he flies home for summer vacation, his mother surprises him with the news that he is being sent to the tiny island of Satawal to spend the summer with his grandfather, Samal, whom he has never met. Samal is "The Navigator," and wishes to teach Gabby the traditional skills of navigation. Although Samal is blind, he can still feel the waves with his body, and predict the weather. At the end of summer, and after an adventurous and dangerous experience at sea, Gabby leaves Satawal with a deeper understanding of himself and of the meaning of friendship, as well as a profound love for his grandfather, his culture, and his heritage.

Steal Away Home. With music. Dramatized by Aurand Harris. Based on the novel by Jane Kristof. Drama.
9 males, 4 females, with doubling. Bare stage with set-pieces pulled on by stage hands. (AP)

This play is about the daring escape of two young slave boys from a South Carolina plantation. With the help of many good people, both black and white, they journey north to join their freed father in Pennsylvania. The play takes us through their many adventures, comic exploits, and narrow escapes. Each episode is bridged by simple spirituals, sung by a choir.

This Is Not a Pipe Dream. Barry Kornhauser. Drama.
2 males, 2 females, 1 gender-neutral stage manager. Unit set incorporating images of artist René Magritte. (AP)

A piece that celebrates art and imagination, this play is loosely based on the work and early life of surrealist artist René Magritte. Young René wants to be an artist, a notion spurned by his father as nothing more than a pipe dream. But the boy is encouraged by his mother before her death, and we see him begin his quest, following his vision into the magic realism of his famous paintings. A play about the true power of dreams and the triumph of the imagination. (Color slides of Magritte's work are available for production use.)

A Thousand Cranes. Kathryn Schultz Miller. Drama.
4 males, 4 females. Area staging. (DPC)

Sadako Saski is now twelve years old. When she was two, the atomic bomb was dropped on her home city of Hiroshima.

She is an excellent athlete and she and her friend Kenji run together daily in preparation for a race. But when Sadako becomes dizzy and falls one day, it is discovered that she has leukemia—caused by the bombing ten years earlier. Kenji, visiting her in the hospital, reminds her of the old story about the crane: Any wish will be granted and Sadako will be well when she finishes folding one thousand origami cranes. As she folds the paper, she calls to her deceased grandmother, and as though in a dream, she is taken to the mountain of her ancestors. She realizes this is where she must stay, even though she has not completed the cranes. "It is better to leave them to others to finish," she is assured by her grandmother. This play is based on a true story: Sadako Saski died October 25, 1955. Her friends and classmates folded the three hundred fifty-six remaining cranes to make a thousand.

Tinker Autumn.   Wil Denson.   Drama.
4 males, 2 females.   1 exterior.   (DPC)

This play takes place in poor rural America. Twelve-year-old Caitlin Moran is illiterate, and thirteen-year-old Peter Crichton is an orphan. They form an unusual alliance in order to fight the system that has placed them outside the mainstream of society. Together they struggle to hang on to their individuality and personal integrity. A compelling play about outcast children containing roles that require a wide range of emotions.

Wiley and the Hairy Man.   Adapted by Jack Stokes.   Fable.
2 males, 1 female, or 3 males or females.   Unit sets.   (DPC)

This play is native folklore. "Outwit the Hairy Man three times and he won't scare you ever again," says Wiley's mammy. Mustering all his courage, the boy sets out for the woods to confront the Hairy Man. The story, which imaginatively intermingles mime with the action, takes us through a series of adventures in which actors become all the props. Wiley ultimately looks fear squarely in the face and outwits it.

Recommended Age-Appropriate Musicals for Junior High Productions

Alice in Concert.   Elizabeth Swados.
6 males, 6 females.   Bare stage.   (French)

An extremely imaginative contemporary rendering of the classic *Alice in Wonderland* story. The actors, dressed in modern rehearsal clothes, impersonate the various Lewis Carroll characters. The music ranges from country-western to calypso.

The Dreams of Jimmy James.   Paul Holmberg.
6 males, 11 females.   Bare stage.   (Baker)

When the curtain rises we suddenly see a scrawny junior high boy of the 1950s hurled onto the stage amidst the sound of boos and Bronx cheers from the wings. Here is a boy who fails miserably in all of his endeavors and sees himself as a big zero. He is, however, infatuated with the queen of his class, Elinor Tomlinson, who is completely unattainable. He escapes into his imagination and becomes everything he's dreamed of being—the king of his school, the idol of all, the coolest of cool. But for every dream, there is a rude awakening. (Music included in script.)

The Great All-American Disaster Musical.   Book by Tim Kelly.   Music and lyrics by Jack Sharkey.
5 males, 6 females, extras, chorus.   One set.   (Baker)

A fast-paced, large-scale spoof. An unscrupulous movie producer cons six major stars into believing they each have the major role in an upcoming movie. Through conniving schemes, hilarious antics and a crafty shooting schedule, he manages to keep them fooled until the movie is completed.

Jigsaw.   Talbot Dewey, Jr.   Music and lyrics by Narcissa Campion.
Large, flexible cast.   Unit sets.   (FP)

An intriguing story about four strangers who find themselves trying to piece together a life-size jigsaw puzzle—one that includes a professional wrestler, an opera singer, an elf, a ballerina, three witches, a bag lady, a scuba diver, and many other fascinating characters. But why? Do the pieces fit? Is there a place for every piece? Is the puzzle complete? And why is the puzzle here in the first place?

Joel and the Wild Goose.   Book, music, and lyrics by Helga Sandburg.
4 males, 2 females, extras.   Area staging.   (DPC)

A touching musical fantasy about a young boy who feels he has nothing he can call his own. One day he encounters a wounded wild goose that's been shot down in his father's woods, and he takes the goose home for a pet. The boy and the goose become so attached to one another that come spring, Joel realizes the bird wants to join his flock. Knowing the goose belongs in the wild, the boy finds the courage to let him go. (This musical can be performed with a female lead, in which case the show is entitled *Nell and the Wild Goose*, and big brother Jim is changed to big sister Nan.)

Left Out.   Sam Abel.   Music and lyrics by Narcissa Campion.
Large, flexible cast.   Unit sets.   (FP)

This musical takes a serious look at peer pressure and prejudice in a private boarding school. In a classroom game about prejudice, left-handed students become the oppressed minorities. But the game starts to turn serious and gets out of hand as the righties wield their authority. The lefties fight back as the righties become blinded by this highly emotional power game trap. Eventually reason prevails, but not without a few tough lessons for the students, their teachers, and their parents.

The Me Nobody Knows.   Robert H. Livingston and Herb Schapiro.   Music by Gary William Friedman and Herb Schapiro.   Lyrics by Will Holt.   Based on the book by Stephen M. Joseph and Herb Schapiro.
Flexible cast of 12.   Area staging.   (French)

A poignant semi-rock musical that began as a collection of writings of ghetto children. The show reveals their inner thoughts, dreams, and observations of life around them. The kids sing, dance, and speak as they mock, enjoy, resent, reject, understand, and love one another. The songs express their innocence, cynicism, and doubts, but for the most part their hope and joy.

Monopoly.   Talbot Dewey, Jr.   Music by Jack and Tom Megan.
Large, flexible cast.   Unit sets.   (FP)

The Monopoly game comes to life in this delightful musical. As a promotional stunt, the wealthy and successful Barker Brothers offer three young people a Monopoly property. As they travel around the board, they meet everyone from the tough, street-wise youths of Baltic Avenue to the uptown sophisticates of Boardwalk. This lighthearted musical raises the issue of socioeconomic differences and examines the decisions young people face in choosing their goals. "Roll the dice for your role in life."

The Red Sneaks.   Elizabeth Swados.
4 males, 4 females.   Unit sets.   (French)

A forceful musical drama immersed in powerful magic. The action takes place in an urban maze of burned-out tenements. A mysterious drifter gives a welfare hotel resident a pair of glittering red sneaks. Whoever wears them has his wishes come true; but the hypnotic power of the sneaks is addictive and even deadly. The allegorical montage of songs, scenes, and monologues makes this show both serious and enjoyable for the cast and audience.

Rock N Roll.   Michael Fingerut and David Cothrell.
12 males, 12 females, extras, chorus.   One permanent set, 2 simple insets.   (Baker)

In this hilarious 1950s teeny-bopper show, we meet the kids of Herbert Hoover High. There's Betsy Lou, who gets stood up by Corndoggie on prom night; Manfred and head cheerleader Darlene, the coolest dancers in town; sad and lonely Duffy and Bumpers, each looking for that special someone; and Corndoggie's rival for Betsy Lou, the super jock and troublemaker Forrest Barrett. These are just a few of the gang of football jocks and cheerleaders from H.H.H. There's also Pops, the understanding adult; rock stars Johnny Sapphire and the Gemstones; and the feared biker gang, Duh Wheels, who rumble with Corndoggie and his buddies. Everything of course turns out happily in the end.

Runaways.   Elizabeth Swados.
11 males, 9 females.   Unit set.   (French)

A musical review about troubled young people. Although the subject is primarily runaways from broken homes, the show makes broader statements about the larger world in which these teenagers live.

Scraps: The Ragtime Girl of Oz.   V. Glasgow Koste.
Inspired by L. Frank Baum.
7 males, 4 females, extras.   Area staging.   (DPC)

In this quirky fantasy musical, a young girl springs to life out of a patchwork quilt. The strange Dr. Pipt created her from his magic powder of life and wants to keep her as his slave. Obstinate and headstrong, Scraps refuses the role and embarks on an adventure with Ojo. As they venture forth, they gather ingredients for a potion to revive Ojo's uncle, who has been temporarily turned to stone in a laboratory accident. They encounter many zany and delightful character along the way—the threatening Woozz, the wise Scrarecrow, and the powerful Princess Ozma, to name a few.

Sneakers.   Judith Weinstein and Arnold Somers.   Music by Elissa Schreiner.   Lyrics by Sunnie Miller.
6 males, 4 females, extras.   Area staging.   (DPC)

After moving to a new city, young Ed is upset about having to leave behind the two most important things that matter in his life—his friends and his Little League status. His spirits lift after his parents buy him a new pair of sneakers which he believes must be magical, for he's never felt better or played better in his life. But his sneakers are stolen and his confidence plummets. He eventually finds the courage to try to make it on his own—and he does! A wonderful contemporary, soft rock musical on finding confidence within ourselves.

T.H.E. Club.   Annette Cantrell Epstein.
Flexible cast of 18, extras.   Area staging.   (Baker)

An inspiring musical about today's environmental problems. Members of the T.H.E. Club (Try Helping the Environment) cover important topics such as acid rain, endangered species, the importance of trees, and the dwindling rain forests. The show's ten songs vary in style—from ballad to ragtime, lighthearted to heartbreaking. A moving and enormously entertaining piece.

Wanna Play?!   Bryan Young and Linda Bergman.   Music by Jeff Rizzo.   Lyrics by Barry Dennen.
Flexible cast of 12.   Area staging.   (Baker)

A musical revue for young teens that deals with the pains, joys, and insanities of early adolescence. The songs deal with a variety of issues facing kids today. There's "Tug of War," about a boy who struggles with the anguish of divorcing parents; "Sisters," a song about sibling rivalry; "It Isn't Fair," in which three girls who are jealous of one another's talents vent their hostility only to discover that each has her own qualities and strong points; and many, many more tunes that junior high students can relate to.

Wee Pals.   Book and lyrics by Ole Kittleson and Morrie Turner.   Music by Norman Boaz.   Based on the comic strip "Wee Pals" created by Morrie Turner.
10 males, 4 females, flexible chorus.   Bare stage w/ props.   (DPC)

The famous comic strip characters come to life in this breezy musical, which shows how fourteen neighborhood friends from various ethnic and religious backgrounds learn to get along with each other in spite of their cultural differences. An exuberant tribute to harmony among people.

Whadda 'Bout My Legal Rights?   Lauren Goldman Marshall and Andrew Duxbury.   Lyrics by Lauren Goldman Marshall, Suzanne Grant, and Andrew Duxbury.
3 males, 3 females, chorus.   Unit sets.   (French)

An entertaining show that teaches young people about their legal rights. The story follows six teenagers as they run into various legal problems ranging from a racist, sexist employer to a school principal who forbids students to wear shorts. Sexual abuse, child support payments, and teen pregnancy are also discussed. A meaningful show that addresses topics concerning young people today, presented in a lively format.

The Writing on the Wall.   David Downing.   Music and lyrics by Martha Rogers.
Large, flexible cast.   Unit sets.   (FP)

"What do I want to do when I grow up?" Miles Elding has decided to become an artist. And in spite of the naysayers who tell him he cannot make money at it, he pursues his dream anyway. He sets off on a wild journey and meets many interesting characters along the way, including two graffiti gangs, the Wall Blasters and the Subway Devils. Together they pool their artistic skills in their efforts to save a building for a group of homeless people and to defeat a corrupt mayor. As Miles continues his search for answers, he discovers some even tougher questions. A funky, bright musical filled with colorful, outrageous characters.

7

Recommended Plays for Senior High School

This appendix lists full-length plays and musicals that contain themes appropriate for high school production as well as challenging roles for teenage actors.

Key to Publishers (see appendix 8 for publishers' addresses):

Baker: Baker's Plays
DPC: Dramatic Publishing Company
DPS: Dramatists Play Service
French: Samuel French
Tams: Tams-Witmark Music Library
R&H: Rodgers and Hammerstein Theatre Library
MTI: Music Theatre International

Classics

Androcles and the Lion.   George Bernard Shaw.   Satire.
14 males, 2 females, 2 extras.   1 interior,
2 exteriors.   (French)

Androcles, a Christian who refuses to hunt or kill, removes a thorn from a grateful lion. Androcles later finds himself a captive with other early Christians in the basement of the Coliseum awaiting death. At the appointed hour, Androcles discovers that the lion to whom he and the others are thrown is the grateful beast whom Androcles befriended.

Antigone.   Sophocles.   Tragedy.
8 males, 4 females.   1 interior.   (French)

Creon decrees that one of the brothers who he believes provoked an evil war be left unburied, denied the rites that would let his soul rest in peace. No one is to bury the body, on pain of death. Antigone, believing in a higher law, covers her brother's body with earth. Creon, her uncle, believing he cannot make an exception for her, has her buried alive for punishment. This act brings about the death of Creon's son who was to marry Antigone. It also provokes Creon's wife to commit suicide, which in time brings about his own downfall. A powerful exploration of the price of sticking to one's principles.

The Birds.   Aristophanes.   Satirical fantasy.
18 or more various male and female characters.   1 interior, 1 exterior.   (French)

The play's heroes, weary of the Athenian social and political atmosphere, decide to build a utopia which they call Nephel-occygia ("Cuckoonebulopolis"). One of the most delightful episodes of the play occurs when a delegation of gods comes to conclude terms with the new city in the sky, which has been impeding sacrifices arising from earth. A lyrical, Uto-pian satire touched by the sadness of the human condition.

The Doctor in Spite of Himself.   Molière.
17th-century farce.
8 males, 4 females.   1 interior, 1 exterior.   (French)

Sganarelle makes his living chopping wood and abuses his wife for amusement. To get revenge, she spreads the rumor that her husband is a brilliant physician who won't reveal his talent unless he is severely punished. His cures appear to be miraculous. A satire on the medical profession.

The Imaginary Invalid. Molière. 17th-century farce.
8 males, 4 females. 1 interior. (French)

Monsieur Arden, a hypochondriac, not only complains about imaginary ills, but also about his huge apothecary bills. He hopes to be free of medical expenses by marrying his daughter Angelique off to a doctor who later proves to be a numbskull. But his daughter is already in love with Cleanthe. Meanwhile, Arden's wife wants to inherit her husband's wealth, and she is determined that Angelique become a nun. At the conclusion, the maid and Arden's brother expose her scheme, and Arden and the doctor as fools.

The Importance of Being Ernest. Oscar Wilde. Farce.
5 males, 4 females. 1 exterior, 2 interiors. (French)

The courtships of Jack and Gwendolen and Algernon and Cecily revolve around a clever case of fabricated mistaken identities. The elaborate plot is ultimately resolved by a fantastical coincidence. In addition to the two couples, this delightful comedy provides several marvelous opportunities for character acting.

The Inspector General. Nikolai Gogol. 19th-century
satirical farce.
15 males, 4 females. 2 interiors. (Baker)

A penniless clerk is mistaken for an important government official. He is wined and dined by the corrupt politicians of a small Russian town. But only after their funds are exhausted is the real inspector discovered.

The Miser. Molière. 17th-century farce.
11 males, 3 females. 1 interior. (French)

The son and daughter of the miser each have a true love and plan to marry. The miser foils their plans by declaring his intentions to marry his son's betrothed for her dowry and to give his daughter to his old wealthy friend, who will demand no dowry. A few frolicking scenes (and a stolen cash box) later, it is revealed that the wealthy old friend is the long-lost father of the boy who is in love with the miser's daughter, as well as the girl who is in love with the miser's son. The miser finally agrees to let his children marry his wealthy friend's new-found children, provided, of course, that the friend pay for the weddings. A stinging commentary on the human cost of avarice.

Pygmalion.   George Bernard Shaw.   Comedy.
6 males, 6 females.   3 interiors, 2 exteriors.   (French)

A phonetics expert bets a friend that he can transform a flower girl with a cockney accent into a well-spoken high society lady. But he never counts on her developing a will of her own . . . .

The Rivals.   Richard Brinsley Sheridan.
Comedy of manners.
8 males, 4 females.   Varied sets.   (French)

Lydia is attracted to Ensign Beverley because she thinks he is a romantic peasant. Her aunt, the hilarious Mrs. Malaprop, wants Lydia to marry the wealthy Jack Absolute. In a humorous twist, it is discovered that Beverley is actually Jack in disguise. Lydia now refuses him because he is wealthy.

School for Scandal.   Richard Brinsley Sheridan.
Comedy of manners.
12 males, 4 females, extras.   Varied sets.   (Baker)

Sir Peter Teagle sees his wife, a simple country maid, become the leader of a school for scandal which meets to gossip and destroy their friends' reputations.

She Stoops to Conquer.
Oliver Goldsmith.   Comedy of manners.
15 males, 4 females.   3 interiors, 1 exterior.   (Baker)

A shy young man travels to visit his intended bride for the first time. He mistakes his betrothed's house for an inn. To make matters worse, he thinks her father is the innkeeper and his fiancée is the maid.

Plays by Shakespeare

As You Like It
Comedy of Errors
Hamlet
A Midsummer Night's Dream
Much Ado About Nothing
Romeo and Juliet
The Taming of the Shrew
Twelfth Night
(Acting editions and streamlined versions are available through Baker and French.)

Dramas

All My Sons.   Arthur Miller.   Drama.
6 males, 4 females.   1 exterior.   (DPS)

During the war Joe Keller and Herbert Deever were partners in a company making parts for aircraft. When defective parts from their shop proved responsible for the death of many men, Deever was sent to jail, but Keller went free and became a wealthy man. The young Keller son, reported missing in action during the war, adds dramatic impact and dominates the action. Herbert Deever's son George returns from the war and finds his father in prison and his partner free. The dramatic climax comes when Joe Keller realizes that he and his partner's company have probably caused the death of his own son.

The Bad Seed.   Maxwell Anderson.   Drama/thriller.
7 males, 5 females.   1 interior.   (DPS)

On the surface, little Rhoda Penmark is all sweetness and charm, but Mrs. Penmark has an uneasy feeling about her. When one of Rhoda's schoolmates mysteriously drowns at a picnic, Rhoda's mother is alarmed. The boy who drowned was the one who had won the penmanship medal that Rhoda felt she deserved. An intriguing suspense story concerning the possibility of inherited evil.

The Barretts of Wimpole Street.   Rudolph Besier.   Drama.
12 males, 5 females.   1 interior.   (DPS)

An ailing Elizabeth Browning lives with her brothers and sisters and a domineering father who rules his house with unbelievable severity. Although her siblings are reconciled to their father's tyranny, Elizabeth has in her a spark of rebellion. The day comes when a young romantic—Robert Browning, who has fallen in love with her through her poetry—bursts upon the Barrett household to declare his love. In spite of Elizabeth's father's attempts to keep her from her suitor, the lovers run away to Italy to marry and begin their life together.

The Crucible.   Arthur Miller.   Drama.
10 males, 11 females.   Single unit set.   (DPS)

A powerful drama about witchcraft in the old New England village of Salem. A young servant girl causes a farmer's wife to be arrested for witchcraft. The girl is brought to court by the farmer to admit the lie. But the monstrous course of deceit and bigotry that follows leads to false accusations against an ever-increasing number of people, including the farmer, who is himself imprisoned and condemned along with his wife.

The Diary of Anne Frank.   Frances Goodrich and Albert Hackett.   Drama.
5 males, 5 females.   1 interior.   (DPS)

Based on the famous diary of a young Jewish girl hiding in an attic with her family to escape the Nazis during World War II. Despite everything, Anne maintains her belief in the goodness of mankind.

Elizabeth the Queen.   Maxwell Anderson.   Romantic drama.
16 males, 7 females, extras.   4 interiors.   (French)

This is a May-December love affair between older Queen Elizabeth and young Essex, who is barely thirty. Elizabeth adores Essex as her lover, but is jealous of Essex the military leader and hero. Elizabeth tries to keep him at court, but Essex longs for glory and power. Through a deceitful plot, he is sent to Ireland where he falls out of favor. When summoned home, he arrives with an army determined to get his way.

An Enemy of the People.   Henrik Ibsen.   Adapted by Arthur Miller.   Drama.
10 males, 3 females.   3 simple interiors.   (DPS)

A small Norwegian town wins fame and wealth through its medicinal springs. The resident physician, Thomas Stock-mann, discovers that the waters are poisoned and reports his findings to the town officials. He is looked upon as a crank who is attempting to ruin the reputation of the town. The physician's family is forced to leave, but do so holding firmly to their belief in the truth.

Flowers for Algernon. David Rogers. Based on the novel by Daniel Keyes. Drama.
10 males, 17 females. Area staging. (DPC)

This is the powerful and tragic story of a retarded man named Charlie, and Algernon, a laboratory mouse. Experimental surgery performed on the mouse increases his intelligence; the same procedure performed on Charlie changes him into a genius. But at the peak of his brilliance, Algernon shows signs of regression. Charlie begins a race against time to retain his own intelligence long enough to save himself and continue his relationship with his teacher Alice Kinnian.

The Glass Menagerie. Tennessee Williams. Drama.
2 males, 2 females. 1 interior. (DPS)

Amanda Wingfield, a worn remnant of Southern society, tries to find meaning in her life by directing the lives of her children. Tom, her son, turns to alcohol and the unrealistic world of movies to escape her nagging. In her mission to find her crippled daughter a husband, Amanda pounces on Tom's friend Jim. In spite of Amanda's meddlesome efforts to push the two together, Jim and Laura get along nicely. But in the end, Jim reveals that he is already engaged. Laura is left to return to her little world of glass animals, and Amanda to the memories of her long-gone youth.

Inherit the Wind. Jerome Laurence and Robert Lee. Drama.
23 males, 7 females, extras. Unit set. (DPS)

A poignant 1920s drama of the Scopes trial, in which a Tennessee schoolteacher was indicted for teaching Darwin's theory of evolution in the schools.

The Lark.   Jean Anouilh.   Adapted by Lillian Hellman. Drama.
15 males, 5 females.   Bare stage, movable platforms.   (DPS)

The play approaches the story of Joan of Arc from both a historical and personal context. By separating the action from the restrictions of time, sequence, and space, Ms. Hellman moves us back and forth in time. The play begins with the trial, and then continues through the young girl's story of the voices which inspired her to save France. The play succeeds in creating a memorable picture of one of history's greatest heroines.

Mary of Scotland.   Maxwell Anderson.   Drama.
22 males, 5 females.   4 interiors, 1 exterior.   (French)

The play begins with Mary's return to England as a queen and ends with her imprisonment by her cousin Elizabeth, the crafty and ambitious queen who seeks to remove from her path a romantic and religious rival.

The Miracle Worker.   William Gibson.   Drama.
7 males, 7 females.   Unit set.   (French)

The poignant dramatization of the real life of Helen Keller. Blind and mute, Helen comes under the care of an Irish girl named Annie Sullivan, who had been born blind herself, and who has been reluctantly hired by the agonized parents of the little girl. After many turbulent and emotionally-charged scenes, Annie realizes that there is a mind waiting to be rescued, and eventually she reaches Helen.

Our Town.   Thornton Wilder.   Drama.
17 males, 7 females, extras.   Bare stage.   (French)

The play takes place in 1901 in Grovers Corner. It is through two neighbors, the Gibbses and the Webbs, that life in this small New Hampshire village is beautifully portrayed with all of its humor, picturesqueness, and pathos.

Outward Bound.   Sutton Vane.   Comedy/drama.
6 males, 3 females.   1 interior.   (French)

A mixed group of personalities makes up the passenger list of an ocean liner whose destination is unknown. It is suddenly revealed that they are all dead and are approaching Judgment Day. Fears and confusion are finally revealed when the Examiner comes aboard to reward virtue and punish vice.

The Rainmaker.   Richard Nash.   Romantic drama.
6 males, 1 female.   Unit set.   (French)

During a severe drought in the West, a father and brothers are worried as much about their plain sister becoming an old maid as they are about their dying cattle. The brothers continue to fail in their schemes to marry her off as the scorching dry heat continues. One day, a sweet-talking gentleman appears and claims to be a rainmaker. He promises to bring rain for $100. The idea is ridiculous, but the family finally agrees. Refreshing and ingratiating, the man turns his charms on the girl and convinces her that she has a special beauty of her own. She and her father believe the fellow can bring rain. The rain comes, and the couple fall in love.

Twelve Angry Men or *Three Angry Women* or *Twelve Angry Jurors.*   Reginald Rose.   Drama/thriller.
15 males, or 15 females, or combined for a mixed cast.
1 interior.   (DPC)

A nineteen-year-old has just stood trial for murdering his father, and twelve jurors are taken into the jury room. What looks like a sure conviction suddenly changes as one of the jurors presses his point about the boy's innocence. This close re-examination of the facts reveals the true character of each juror as well. The murder is re-enacted and a new murder threat surfaces. The heated arguments and short tempers of twelve angry people finally lead to a verdict that will keep the audience on the edge of their seats.

Comedies and Farces

The Admirable Crichton.   James M. Barrie.   Satire.
13 males, 12 females, extras.   2 interiors.   (French)

Once a month, the Earl of Loam invites all of his servants into the drawing room where they are treated as social equals—much to the distaste of Crichton, the butler who knows his place. Crichton accompanies the Earl, his three daughters, and high society friends on a yachting party. When they become marooned on a desert island, Crichton takes command, and through his resourcefulness he wins their respect. Many of the women vie for his affection, and he chooses Lady Mary to be his wife. Unfortunately, they are rescued and Crichton gives up his love. All revert to their former positions on their return to England.

Ah, Wilderness!   Eugene O'Neill.   Comedy.
9 males, 6 females.   2 interiors, 1 exterior.   (French)

An ordinary, small-town, 1906 American family with average problems are concerned about the emotional intensity of their eighteen-year-old son Richard, a rebellious high school senior who hates money and reads Swinburne, Shaw, Wilde, and Omar Khayyam. After his girlfriend is forced to break up with him, he rebels and puts his family through a variety of misadventures before everything returns to normal and the boy and girl are united.

The Madwoman of Chaillot.   Jean Giraudoux.
Comedy/drama.
17 males, 8 females.   1 interior, 1 exterior.   (DPS)

At the Café Chez Francis, a group of promoters plot to tear up Paris for oil that a prospector believes he has located in the neighborhood. A "madwoman," who insists the world is being turned into an unhappy place by the world's financiers and other money-worshipping materialists, brings together these despoilers of the earth for a tea party. There she has them tried and condemned to extermination in order to save Paris and the world.

The Man Who Came to Dinner.   Moss Hart and George S. Kaufman.   Comedy.
15 males, 9 females.   1 interior.   (DPS)

After dining at the Stanleys', Sheridan Whiteside slips on their doorstep and breaks a hip. Confined to a wheelchair, the irascible invalid turns the household upside down with an assortment of strange friends, transatlantic phone calls, and strange gifts from well-wishers, including a large mummy case that is used in a clever ruse to get rid of a guest. After six weeks, Whiteside finally leaves the Stanleys' house, but seconds later a crash is heard—he has slipped and fallen again!

The Matchmaker.   Thornton Wilder.   Farce.
9 males, 7 females.   4 interiors.   (French)

A rich merchant from Yonkers hires Dolly Levi to arrange a marriage for him. Dolly subsequently gets entangled with two of his menial clerks, an assortment of young and lovely ladies, and a head waiter. And after a series of hide-and-seek scenes and a hilarious climax of complications in an expensive restaurant, everyone gets straightened out romantically, even the merchant—who ends up marrying the matchmaker!

The Mouse That Roared.   Leonard Wibberley and Christopher Sergel.   Comedy.
14 males, 16 females, extras if desired (doubling possible).
Area staging.   (DPC)

The Duchess Gloriana is sovereign of the tiny, near-bankrupt country of Grand Fenwick, founded centuries ago by a roving band of English bowmen. She decides to declare war on America, for as recent history suggests, the surest way to wealth is to lose a war with the United States, whose habit it is to send money and aid to the vanquished. When the Duchess's declaration of war is taken to be a prank, Tully Bascom and his bowmen launch an attack. Ironically, Grand Fenwick wins the war and finds itself in an awkward position.

Mr. Pim Passes By.   A. A. Milne.   Light comedy.
3 males, 4 females.   1 interior.   (French)

The name-dropping Mr. Pim gives a lady the impression that her first husband is still alive, much to the consternation of her pompous second husband. But when the truth is finally discovered, the lady uses it to manipulate her second husband.

A Raisin in the Sun.   Lorraine Hansberry.   Comedy/drama.
7 black males, 3 black females, 1 black child.
1 interior.   (French)

The setting is Chicago's Southside black ghetto during the 1950s. Involved are the dreams and conflicts of the Younger family spanning three generations. African-American identity, pride, and power, coupled with the family's strength and links to Black Africa, all culminate in the family's refusal at the end to sacrifice their dignity to the demands of a hostile, greedy, racist society.

Rhinoceros. Eugene Ionesco. Absurd comedy.
11 males, 6 females, extras. 1 exterior,
2 interiors. (French)

One Sunday morning, a small town is suddenly besieged by a roaring rhinoceros. The excitement of the townsfolk, however, is not due to the animal's presence, but to whether it has one or two horns and whether its variety is Asiatic or African. As the people complacently argue these points, they are, one by one, turned into rhinos themselves, as the main character looks on in horror. A fierce commentary on the absurdity of the human condition.

The Romancers. Edmond Rostand. English version by Barrett H. Clark. Romantic comedy.
5 males, 1 female. 1 exterior. (French)

Two young people whose parents wish them to marry refuse to accept their parents' plans. In order to draw the couple together, the fathers pretend to hate one another. Their plot succeeds, but only after the boy and girl run away and return disillusioned.

The Skin of Our Teeth. Thornton Wilder. Satirical fantasy.
5 males, 5 females, many extras. 1 interior,
1 exterior. (French)

The Antrobus family through many generations have narrowly survived fire, flood, pestilence, the Ice Age, and the double feature. This crazy adventurous play is tangible proof of faith in mankind.

Solid Gold Cadillac. Howard Teichmann and George S. Kaufman. Comedy.
11 males, 6 females. Varied stylized sets. (DPS)

A little old lady who owns ten shares of a manufacturing empire called General Products attends a stockholders meeting. She is permitted to speak. After informing the board members that she has read every page of the annual report, she begins to asks very pointed questions about the board's inflated salaries. Worried by her inquiries, the board decides to hire her to keep her quiet, but she is not so easily controlled. After the little old lady uncovers the mess the current board is making of the business, the former owner fights to regain control of the company and does so with her help.

Teahouse of the August Moon. John Patrick. Based on the novel by Vern Sneider. Comedy.
18 males, 8 females, 3 children. Multiple interiors and exteriors. (DPS)

This is the story of an army officer stationed in Okinawa during the island occupation in World War II. His duties are to teach the natives about democracy, and there is a stupid and stern colonel breathing down his neck making sure he is strictly following army procedure as outlined in the Manual of Occupation. The young officer, however, is won over by the ingenious charm of the natives and soon becomes the owner of a Grade A geisha girl. The materials sent to him for constructing a school are used to build a teahouse. To help boost the village economy he sells local potato brandy to the surrounding Army and Navy officers' clubs. The colonel shows up to inspect the village on the same day the teahouse opens. It appears the officer is sure to be court martialed and the colonel demoted, but word arrives from Washington that the village is the most progressive on the island and all is forgiven.

You Can't Take It with You.   Moss Hart and George S. Kaufman.   Comedy.
9 males, 7 females, extras.   1 interior.   (DPS)

The delightfully zany Sycamore family, each pursuing their own hobbies and living an unorthodox life, nearly break up their daughter Alice's romance with Tony Kirby when he and his stuffy parents are invited for dinner, but arrive at the Sycamore home on the wrong night.

Age-Appropriate Full-Length Plays for Teenage Actors

There is a growing body of plays written specifically for the high school actor; many deal with contemporary issues confronting young adults today. The following plays have been selected for their substantive material, challenging roles, minimal scenery, and strong audience appeal.

And Stuff. . . .   Peter Dee.   Drama.
Flexible cast.   Bare stage.   (Baker)

In this sequel to *Voices from the High School*, a series of monologues and short scenes brings to light the teen experience of living and surviving "now" in this country. The play reveals the joys and difficulties of becoming an adult. The play deliberately contains more challenging and difficult roles than its predecessor.

Ashes, Ashes, All Fall Down.   Joseph Robinette.
Optional music by James R. Shaw.   Drama.
6 males, 4 females.   Area staging.   (DPC)

At a Who concert in Cincinnati, six young people were
crushed to death by the crowd trying to get in. This drama
studies their lives. It also deals with four other people who
are attempting to discover the reasons for their deaths. Although serious in nature, the play is full of hope and humor
as it examines other relevant themes such as hero worship,
estranged relationships, and the need for family.

Babies Having Babies.   Kathryn Montgomery and Jeffrey
Auerbach.   Drama.
2 males, 5 females.   1 interior with side platforms.   (Baker)

A frank, sensitive, humorous play about young women facing
the prospect of unplanned, unwanted pregnancy. Each of the
characters reveals her own dreams of achievement and her
plans for what is now an uncertain future. A powerful play
exposing the inner conflicts young women must cope with.
More often than not, they face their problems alone, with
little help from adults, and no understanding from their peers.

Beloved Friend.   Nancy Pahl Gilsenan.   Drama.
13 males, 9 females, integrated.
Multiple simple sets.   (DPC)

Kristen, a high school student, and Rachel, a Rhodesian girl
of the same age, become pen pals. Through the years of their
friendship they share the joys and sorrows of their lives. The
contrast is dramatic when the affluence of American life is
compared to the poverty and indignities of life in Rhodesia
(now Zimbabwe). Rachel gets an education and in later years
becomes her country's Minister of Education. When she looks

up her friend Kristen on a visit to America, she find her in a coma suffering from multiple sclerosis. In a final and touching scene at the end, Kristen is awakened by Rachel's voice and the two pen pals share a delicious moment of contact.

Black Elk Speaks.   John Neihardt and Christopher Sergel. Drama.
Flexible cast of 16, with doubling, many more as desired.
Bare stage with several levels.   (DPC)

An entirely authentic play that describes in a passionate, mystical language how the Plains Indians were destroyed and their lands taken away. The details of the destruction are vividly depicted and told by Black Elk and his cousin Crazy Horse. The excitement mounts as the play rapidly shows a way of life that is no more and also shows it as it could be for all people.

Dino.   Reginald Rose.   Drama.
7 males, 11 females, extras.   Divided interior set.   (DPC)

A complicated and difficult seventeen-year-old, Dino has just finished a four-year sentence in reform school. The story centers around the efforts of Dino's tough, competent, and caring parole officer who keeps this troubled youth from turning into a confirmed criminal.

The Fifth Sun.   Nicholas Patricca.   Drama.
Mixed cast of 6 to 14 actors.   Area staging.   (DPC)

This powerful ensemble piece revolves around the 1980 assassination of Oscar Romero, Archbishop of San Salvador, a man who left a vision of morality to his people. The play presents the story of the people and an ordinary man changed by circumstance into a courageous leader. Elements of ancient tomb rituals, Mayan temple dramas, and medieval morality plays are cleverly entwined to create a touching contemporary play.

I Never Saw Another Butterfly. Celeste Raspanti. Drama. 4 males, 7 females, 4 children, extras. Area staging. (DPC)

A survivor of the Nazi death camps describes the stirring events at a way station called Terezin where Jewish children were held before their shipment to their final destination. At Terezin they were taught even though there was nothing to teach with; they were given hope when there was no hope. There were no butterflies at Terezin, but the butterfly became a symbol of defiance in the children's drawings, giving them the strength to live on and play while awaiting deportation.

In the Middle of Grand Central Station. Nancy Pahl Gilsenan. Drama. 6 males, 6 females, extras. Area staging. (DPC)

This play examines the search of a young runaway to find her place in a disintegrating social system. From a broken home, to city psychiatric wards, through residential treatment centers, fifteen-year-old Mary de Silva has been on the run—until she reaches the world's most famous train station. Here she finds freedom, friends, and a kind of dignity. But drugs and despair create a loss of hope no adolescent should ever experience. A play about survival and what happens to kids with hopes and dreams when the odds are against them.

The Inner Circle. Patricia Loughrey. Drama. 2 males, 2 females. 1 interior. (Baker)

A boy named Mark experimented with drugs only once in his life, sharing a needle with a friend. The drug experience seems behind him—until he discovers he has AIDS. As Mark battles with the disease, we see his friends build a capsule of memories and images of their times together that will stay with them all of their lives.

Kicking Back. Peter Dee. Play with music.
6 males, 8 females. Representational sets. (Baker)

Told with the stark and powerful language of the streets, this provocative work deals with the teen experience of the 1990s. A group of teenagers want their anti-drug song heard at a local teen club. But drug dealers in the area attempt to sabotage their efforts by threatening to kill one of the teen's relatives. A powerful message portrayed with humor, music, and an understanding of today's teens.

The Late Great Me. David Rogers. Adapted from the novel by Sandra Scoppettone. Drama.
10 males, 12 females, extras. Area staging. (DPC)

This is a hard-hitting play about teenage alcoholism. Geri Peters, a shy, insecure girl, can't believe David Townsend, one of the best looking boys at school, is attracted to her. Sensing the weak point in her character, he leads her into alcoholism. A sensitive and at times humorous play with a firm and positive point of view.

Makin' It. Cynthia Mercati. Comedy.
10 males, 13 females. 1 interior/flexible set. (Baker)

A quick-witted, open, and up-front play on surviving high school. Whether they're facing adult pressure, peer pressure, the fear of being considered a nerd, a geek, a burn-out, or the fear of being unpopular, the characters in the play are all honest, real, and recognizable as they struggle through this important period of their lives.

Painted Face.   Molly G. Bass & Sylvia B. Hoffmire.
Drama.
7 males, 6 females, 1 voice.   Unit set.   (Baker)

Khaki Manders is seventeen years old, the daughter every parent dreams of having—attractive, popular, and talented. She comes from a supportive, affluent family and is happy and grateful for all her good fortune. But she hides a dark, painful secret—her despair. Khaki Manders may never reach her eighteenth birthday because she is suicidal. A true-to-life play that takes a hard look at the third highest killer of teenagers today.

Revenge of the Space Panda or Binky Rudich and the Two-Speed Clock.   David Mamet with music by Alaric Jans.
Comedy.
6 males, 3 females, with doubling.   Multiple simple sets.
(DPC)

Binky Rudich and his friends tinker with a two-speed clock with the idea that time on Earth does not move at the same time all the time. They believe there is another speed, a slower speed, and if they could find it, everything would stand still on Earth and everyone would spin off! And they do! They land in Crestview, Fourth World in the Goolangong System, ruled by George Topax and guarded by the Great Space Pandas. This insane comedy dealing with an equally insane idea is filled with intrigue and humor.

Second Hand Kid.   Craig Sodaro.   Drama.
3 males, 4 females.   1 interior.   (DPC)

Connie D'Amato decides to take in Lisa, a foster child who turns out to be a sixteen-year-old repeat offender with a history of drug addiction and abuse. Family conflicts ensue, but only Papa, Connie's father-in-law, seems to be able to reach her. Throughout the play we see a deeply troubled young girl struggling to find respect for herself, who has been rejected by the world, and searching for her place in it. This is a powerful play about the decisions and choices young people must make and those they force on others.

Voices from the High School. Peter Dee. Drama. Flexible cast. Bare stage with pieces. (Baker)

A popular high school play, this series of vignettes reflects the joys and problems of growing up too fast in America. The monologues and two-character scenes deal with such issues as love, friendship, teacher/student rapport, alcoholism, teen pregnancy, suicide, and a lot more.

Musicals

This sampling of famous Broadway and Off-Broadway musicals has broad audience appeal. The plays contain roles that can readily be handled by teen actors and deal with subject matter that is appropriate for high school productions.

Annie (MTI)
Annie Get Your Gun (R&H)
Anything Goes (Tams)
The Boyfriend (MTI)
Bye, Bye Birdie (Tams)
Carnival (Tams)
Dames at Sea (French)
The Fantasticks (MTI)
Fiddler on the Roof (MTI)
Flower Drum Song (R&H)
Funny Girl (Tams)
George M (Tams)

Good News (French)
Grease (French)
Guys and Dolls (MTI)
High Spirits (Tams)
How to Succeed in Business without Really Trying (MTI)
Joseph and the Amazing Technicolor Dreamboat (MTI)
1776 (MTI)
Li'l Abner (Tams)

Little Mary Sunshine
   (French)
Little Shop of Horrors
   (French)
The Music Man (MTI)
My Fair Lady (Tams)
No, No, Nanette (Tams)
Oklahoma! (R&H)
Oliver! (Tams)
Once Upon a Mattress
   (R&H)
*One Hundred and Ten
   in the Shade* (Tams)

Paint Your Wagon (Tams)
The Pajama Game (MTI)
Pippin (MTI)
Prom Queens Unchained
   (French)
The Secret Garden (French)
The Sound of Music (MTI)
South Pacific (R&H)
*The Unsinkable Molly
   Brown* (MTI)
West Side Story (MTI)
The Wiz (French)

8

Play Publisher Directory

All of the following publishers will mail their play catalogues to schools free of charge. The Baker's play catalogue includes an invaluable resource directory listing suppliers of theatrical goods and services.

Play Catalogues

Anchorage Press, Inc.
P.O. Box 8067
New Orleans, LA 70182

504-283-8868

Art Craft Publishing Co.
232 Dows Building
Cedar Rapids, IA 52406

319-364-6311

Baker's Play Publishing Co.
100 Chauncy Street
Boston, MA 02111

617-482-1280
FAX: 617-482-7613

Contemporary Drama Service
Meriwether Publishing Ltd.
Box 7710-U
Colorado Springs, CO 80933

719-594-4422
FAX: 719-594-9916
Orders: 800-937-5297

The Dramatic Publishing Co.
P.O. Box 129
311 Washington Street
Woodstock, IL 60098

815-338-7170
FAX: 815-338-8981
Orders: 800-448-7469
FAX: 800-334-5302

Dramatists Play Service, Inc.
440 Park Avenue South
New York, NY 10016

212-683-8960
FAX: 212-213-1539

Eldridge Publishing Co. P.O. Box 216 Franklin, OH 45005	800-447-8243 FAX: 513-746-6766
Encore Performance Publishing P.O. Box 692 Orem, UT 84057	801-225-0605 Order: 800-927-1605
The Freelance Press P.O. Box 548 Dover, MA 02030	508-785-1260
I. E. Clark, Inc. Saint John's Road Box 246 Schulenburg, TX 78956	409-743-3232 FAX: 409-743-4765
Music Theatre International 545 8th Avenue New York, NY 10018	212-868-6668 FAX: 212-643-8465
Pioneer Drama Service P.O. Box 22555 Denver, CO 80222	303-759-4297 FAX: 303-759-0475 Hot Line: 800-333-7262
Players Press, Inc. P.O. Box 1132 Studio City, CA 91614	818-789-4980
Rogers & Hammerstein Theatre Library 1633 Broadway Suite 3801 New York, NY 10019	212-541-6900 FAX: 212-586-6155
Samuel French, Inc. 45 West 25th Street New York, NY 10010	212-206-8990 FAX: 212-206-1429
Samuel French, Inc. (western states) 7623 Sunset Boulevard Hollywood, CA 90046	213-876-0570 FAX: 213-876-6822

Tams-Witmark Music Library   212-688-2525
560 Lexington Avenue   FAX: 212-688-3232
New York, NY 10022   Orders: 800-221-7196
                                  NY only: 800-522-2181

Magazine Publications of Plays

Plays, the Drama Magazine   Tel.: 617-423-3157
for Young People
120 Boylston Street
Boston, MA 02116

Dramatics Magazine   Tel.: 513-559-1996
3368 Central Parkway
Cincinnati, OH 45225

GLOSSARY

A cappella   Without musical accompaniment.

Backdrop   A large cloth painted to resemble landscape or other desired scenery suspended from a batten or rod.

Blocking   The director's planned movement for the actors within the staging area.

Book   Script.

Callbacks   The final audition from which the cast will be selected.

Characterization   The process of developing and understanding the personality, motives, and behavior of a character in portraying a role.

Commedia dell'arte   A style of improvisational comic theater that flourished during the Renaissance; it was performed on a simple platform usually in public streets.

Corner block   Triangle made of quarter-inch plywood used to reinforce the corners of a flat.

Downstage   Stage area nearest the audience.

Flat   The basic element of stage scenery; a rectangular wooden frame covered with muslin and then painted.

Follow book   To follow the scripted dialogue of a scene or play as it is being performed by the actors.

Gelling lights   The process of cutting and placing gelatin (trans-

223

parent colored sheets) into the gel frame of stage lights to create special color or mood effects.

Go cue A signal to execute a sound effect, or a lighting, curtain, or set change.

God chart Common name for a rehearsal overview chart containing the first week's rehearsal schedule through the post-production strike.

Keystone Rectangle made of quarter-inch plywood used to reinforce the joints of a flat.

Lash cleat Metal cleat fastened to the stiles of a flat, used for holding flats together by lashing.

Lash line Quarter-inch sash cord used for lashing flats together.

Mask To hide something from the audience's view.

Modeling The process of using others as examples for discovering appropriate patterns of behavior for a role.

Neuro-Linguistic Programming A system for producing a desired state of mind and its correlating behavior; an effective tool for training young actors.

Off book To rehearse without script in hand; i.e., to have dialogue memorized.

Proscenium stage Stage with a permanent framed opening.

Promptbook Book containing script, blocking notations, technical warnings and cues, production charts, or any other technical-information required to produce a play.

Prompting lines The process of following the script during rehearsals and providing actors with missed words or forgotten lines of dialogue.

Props Stage properties, i.e., set furnishings including tables, chairs, furniture, drapes, etc., and any items used or handled by the actors.

Rails The top and bottom crosspieces of a flat.

Returns   Flats placed parallel to the footlights and attached to the downstage edges of a set; can be carried off into the wings behind the tormentors.

Royalty   Money paid to a playwright for permission to produce a play.

Run lines   To practice lines with fellow actors as a means of learning dialogue.

Run-through   The rehearsal of an entire scene or play without interruption.

Scrim   A loose-weave cloth used for special scenery effects; transparent when lighted from the back and opaque when lighted from the front.

Special   Spotlight used to create a special effect or mood in a play.

Stage brace   Adjustable hardwood brace with a hook on one end used to hold scenery in place.

Stage business   An actor's subtle actions or activities, such as pencil-tapping, paging through a magazine, knitting, filing fingernails, etc.

Stage cleat   A metal plate with a hole on one side to accommodate the hook of a stage brace.

Stage left   Playing area to the left of an actor facing the audience.

Stage right   Playing area to the right of an actor facing the audience.

Stage screw   A large metal screw with a butterfly head, used to anchor stage braces to the floor.

Stiles   The vertical side pieces of a flat.

Strike   To take down the set after the run of the show.

Striking props and sets   Removing objects, furniture, and scenery from the stage.

Teaser   Overhead drape used to mask the fly area and first border of lights; also used to adjust the height of the proscenium opening.

Tie-off cleat   A two-holed metal cleat placed at a slight angle to the stile for tying off the lash line used to hold flats together.

Toggle rail   The cross member located between the top and bottom rails of a flat.

Tormentors   A series of solid-colored flats placed on either side of the stage directly behind the teaser to hide the wing area from the audience's view.

Upstage   Stage area farthest from the audience.

Visualization   Mental imaging; an effective technique in creating a role.

Wing and fly space   Offstage areas directly above (fly area) and to the left and right (wings) of the playing area.

SOURCES

Boleslavsky, Richard. *Acting: The First Six Lessons*. New York: Theatre Arts Books, 1949.

Brockett, Oscar G. *History of the Theatre*. 6th ed. Boston: Allyn and Bacon, 1990.

Buerki, F. A. *Stagecraft for Nonprofessionals*. 3d ed. Madison: University of Wisconsin Press, 1983.

Corson, Richard. *Stage Makeup*. 8th ed. Englewood Cliffs, NJ: Prentice Hall, 1990.

Cummings, Richard. *Simple Makeup for Young Actors*. Boston: Plays, Inc., 1990.

Fuchs, Theodore. *Home-Built Lighting Equipment: For the Small Stage*. New York: Samuel French, 1939.

Garvin, James P. *Learning How to Kiss a Frog: Advice for Those Who Work with Pre- and Early Adolescents*. Rowley, MA: New England League of Middle Schools, 1988.

Hagen, Uta, and Haskel Frankel. *Respect for Acting*. New York: Macmillan, 1973.

Hake, Herbert V. *Here's How: A Basic Stagecraft Book*. New York: Samuel French, 1958.

Hall, Karen M. "Performing for the Musical Theatre." *Musical Show* 33, no.1 (February 1993): 3–4.

Hartnoll, Phyllis. *The Theatre: A Concise History*. Rev. ed. New York: Thames and Hudson, 1989.

Highet, Gilbert. *The Art of Teaching*. New York: Random House, Vintage Books, 1989.

Holtje, Adrienne K., and Grace A. Mayr. *Putting on the School Play: A Complete Handbook*. West Nyack, NY: Parker Publishing, 1980.

Lounsbury, Warren C. *Theatre Backstage from A to Z.* 3d ed. Seattle: University of Washington Press, 1992.

Miller, James Hull. *Stage Lighting in the Boondocks.* 3d ed. Colorado Springs: Meriwether Publishing, 1987.

Moore, Sonia. *The Stanislavski System: Revised Edition of the Stanislavski Method.* New York: Viking Press, 1965.

Motter, Charlotte K. *Theatre in High School: Planning, Teaching, Directing.* Lanham, MN: University Press of America, 1984.

Ommanney, Katharine Anne, and Harry H. Schanker. *The Stage and the School.* 5th ed. St. Louis: McGraw-Hill, 1982.

Paperbound Books in Print. New York: R. R. Bowker. Published biannually

Parker, W. Oren, and Harvey K. Smith. *Scenic Design and Stage Lighting.* 6th ed. New York: Holt, Rinehart and Winston, 1990.

Reid, Francis. *The Stage Lighting Handbook.* 4th ed. New York: Theatre Arts Books, 1992.

Robbins, Anthony. *Unlimited Power.* New York: Fawcett Columbine, 1986.

Russell, Douglas A. *Stage Costume Design: Theory, Technique, and Style.* 2d ed. Englewood Cliffs, NJ: Prentice Hall, 1985.

Schlusberg, Julian S. *Lessons for the Stage: An Approach to Acting.* Hamden, CT: Archon Books, 1994.

Spolin, Viola. *Improvisation for the Theater: A Handbook of Teaching and Directing Techniques.* 4th ed. Evanston, IL: Northwestern University Press, 1990.

Strong, William S. *The Copyright Book: A Practical Guide.* 3d ed. Cambridge, MA: MIT Press, 1990.

Tanner, Fran Averett. *Basic Drama Projects.* 5th ed. Pocatello, ID: Clark Publishing, 1987.

Young, John Wray, and Margaret Mary Young. *How to Produce the Play: The Complete Production Handbook.* Woodstock, IL: Dramatic Publishing, 1960.

Zortman, Bruce. *Promptbook: A Comprehensive Guide for Teaching Adolescents the Techniques of Acting.* El Paso: Firestein Books, 1991.

———. *TechOne: A Comprehensive Guide for Teaching Adolescents the Skills of Technical Theatre.* El Paso: Firestein Books, 1992.